PREGNANCY BOOK

in consultation with

Robert D. Auerbach, M.D., F.A.C.O.G.

Associate Clinical Professor
Department of Obstetrics, Gynecology and Reproductive Sciences
Yale University School of Medicine

Senior Vice President and Chief Medical Officer
CooperSurgical, Inc.

Illustrator:
Amy Millar

Graphic Design:
Alicia Goff
Chris Rubino

Copyright 2011 by Budlong Press, a CooperSurgical Company • Trumbull, CT 06611
First published 1963; Thirty-fourth edition, revised 2007
ISBN Number 978-1-934052-10-5 • Printed in the United States

Chapter 13: Becoming a mother 136
How to tell when labor begins. When to call your clinician. What happens
during labor. Apgar. Episiotomy. Analgesics and anesthetics. Kinds of birth.
Vaginal birth after cesarean (VBAC). Preterm labor and delivery. Induced
labor. Fetal monitoring. Certified Nurse Midwives.

Chapter 14: After delivery 155
The uterus (womb). Your breasts. The nursing mother. How long
should you nurse. The non-nursing mother. Smoking and your baby.
Other concerns after delivery. Postpartum blues. Depression. Psychosis.
Circumcision for boy babies. Visitors. A few pointers about hygiene.

Chapter: 15 Going home 165
Postpartum exercises. Diet. Return of menstruation. Sex relations
and family planning. Emergency contraception. Your postpartum checkup.
Signs and symptoms to report after delivery. Some advice about your first
weeks at home.

Chapter 16: Working at motherhood 172
The baby's weight. Baby's sleeping pattern. The soft spot. Jaundice.
Caring for the umbilical cord and circumcision. Birth certificate.
Enjoy your baby.

Appendix

Pregnancy Preface

*Y*OU ARE URGED TO READ THIS PRENATAL BOOK in its entirety. As you progress through the different stages of your pregnancy you should review and reread those sections of this book that are relevant to you at that time. You'll find it to be a helpful source of information throughout your pregnancy.

One of the most important things you can do for your baby is to follow a healthy lifestyle and seek early and regular prenatal care.

There are several important facts, among others mentioned in this publication, you should be aware of and report to your clinician or other health professional as soon as possible.

For example, report:

1. Exposure to German measles (rubella) or other infectious diseases. Infection with measles, mumps or German measles during pregnancy can cause birth defects in the fetus. The recommended waiting period, if you have not had German measles, is to be vaccinated against this disease at least 28 days before becoming pregnant, according to the Centers for Disease Control and Prevention (CDC). Live vaccines to prevent these and other diseases, may be harmful to the fetus. (See new recommendations for German measles page 31 point 5.)

2. Exposure to, or past history of, a sexually transmitted disease such as human papilloma virus (HPV), chlamydia, gonorrhea syphilis or other STD.

3. Whether you or the father have AIDS (Acquired Immune Deficiency Syndrome) or have tested positive for HIV.

4. A family history of any genetic diseases such as Tay-Sachs Disease, Sickle-Cell Anemia, Down Syndrome, Cystic Fibrosis or Diabetes.

5. If your mother took diethylstilbestrol (DES) while she was pregnant with you.

You should avoid:

- All drugs, prescription and non-prescription, unless your clinician, knowing you are pregnant, specifically recommends or prescribes such a drug. You should not stop taking medication for pre-existing medical conditions such as, diabetes, heart disease, epilepsy, without consulting your physician. He/she may recommend adjusting your dosage or changing your medication during pregnancy.

- The drug Accutane® (Isotretinoin), which is prescribed for cystic acne, should be discontinued at least one month before becoming pregnant. If you are taking this drug and suspect you may be pregnant, notify your clinician immediately. Retin A, which is molecularly similar to Accutane, may also present a risk of birth defects.

The Food and Drug Administration (FDA) now recommends that a woman provide documentation for a negative pregnancy test to her pharmacist before a prescription for Accutane is filled.

There are other drugs which are known to be teratogens (agents that can cause birth defects), that may have to be discontinued before planning or becoming pregnant.

Do Not Take:

- Contraceptive drugs: discontinue one to two months before becoming pregnant.

- Vitamin A: Studies at Boston University School of Medicine indicate that women who take large amounts of preformed vitamin A prior to becoming pregnant or during the first few months of pregnancy, appear more likely to bear children with birth defects. Taking vitamin A supplements during pregnancy is not recommended according to medical publications. (See pages 75-76 for recommended daily vitamin needs.)

- Soriatane: Prescribed for psoriasis, the use of this medication should be discontinued at least three years before becoming pregnant.

- Any vaccine made from live viruses, such as those for measles mumps or chicken pox should be avoided for at least three months before becoming pregnant and during pregnancy.

See page 179 for additional agents known to be harmful to fetus.

Accutane® is a registered trademark of Roche Pharmaceuticals.

You should avoid hot baths, saunas, hot tubs or other facilities that elevate maternal body temperature particularly during the first 3 months of your pregnancy (see pages 105-106).

Radiation is used in some jobs in the form of X-rays to diagnose and treat disease. High doses of radiation can lower fertility in men and women and can affect the fetus. The amount of radiation exposure in a chest X-ray will not affect fertility or the fetus. Radiation to treat disease such as cancer can be harmful. (See pages 103-104 for more information on radiation.)

Recent Study Findings

Because most women are not aware immediately that they are pregnant and neural tube defects occur during the first month of pregnancy, the Centers for Disease Control and Prevention (CDC) in Atlanta, Georgia, issued a recommendation that all women of childbearing age in the United States take 0.4 mg of folic acid per day to reduce the risk of having a baby affected with spina bifida or other neural tube defects. A study reported in the August 1995 issue of Lancet, an English medical journal, found that women who took multivitamins containing folic acid at the time they conceived, substantially reduced their infant's risk for oral or facial defects such as cleft palate and lip.

Women who have given birth to a baby with a neural tube defect are at higher risk of it recurring in a subsequent pregnancy. For this reason they are advised to take 10 times more folic acid than is routinely recommended, 4 mg daily for 1 month before becoming pregnant and during the first 3 months of the pregnancy. These women should take a folic acid vitamin alone rather than a multivitamin containing folic acid. In order to get enough folic acid from a multivitamin, a woman would get an overdose of other vitamins. It is important to discuss this with your physician before taking any vitamins or other medication.

The National Institutes of Health sponsored a study which found that women who took a daily folic acid supplement of at least 400 micrograms during the first six weeks of their pregnancy, reduced their risk of having a baby with a congenital heart defect. A mandate by the Food and Drug Administration (FDA) to fortify grain products (breads) with folic acid may prevent miscarriages as well as lowering the risk of neural tube defects.

If you are less than six weeks pregnant, you can take a folic acid supplement rather than your multivitamin containing folic acid because folic acid alone is less likely to upset your stomach. It is very important that you have sufficient folic acid early in your pregnancy.

Researchers have found that men who do not eat enough fruits and vegetables rich in vitamin C were more likely to have damaged DNA, the genetic material found in chromosomes. This could increase the risks of birth defects, genetic diseases and/or cancer in their children. It is therefore prudent for a man to follow the government's dietary guide (see food pyramid page 66). This is even more important in smokers because vitamin C in the body is dissipated by tobacco use.

Recently published research, spanning 12 years of study, suggests the alcohol intake of men prior to mating can result in abnormalities of the fetus even if the woman does not drink any alcohol.

HIV infected women who are pregnant, including those who have no symptoms of AIDS, treated with medications against HIV are much less likely to pass the AIDS virus on to the fetus. The drug(s) should be given to the HIV positive woman during her pregnancy, labor and delivery, and the baby must take the drug(s) during the first six weeks of life. There is a test called enzyme-linked immunosorbent assay (ELISA) available to detect if your blood contains HIV antibodies, a sign of infection. Discuss this with your clinician. Some states require an HIV test as part of your routine blood work.

Good health and a normal or near normal weight before becoming pregnant will help you throughout your pregnancy. The early weeks of pregnancy, even before the pregnancy is confirmed, are crucial ones for the embryo/fetus (the first eight weeks after conception the fertilized egg is called an embryo, thereafter, until birth, it is called a fetus). It is during these early weeks that the organs are being formed. It is at this stage, as well as later in the pregnancy, that substances such as alcohol, nicotine, illicit drugs and certain medications can be most dangerous to the embryo/fetus.

Should you have any questions regarding your pregnancy or information found in this book speak with your clinician or other healthcare professional.

Chapter 1 Examination for pregnancy

*P*REGNANCY CAN BE AN EXCITING, fulfilling, delightful time. In the months ahead, you will be undergoing a variety of changes—changes in the way your body looks, changes in the way you feel, changes in your daily activities, and changes in your wardrobe. These changes will be exciting ones, but they may also be cause for concern and anxiety.

The purpose of this book is to help you understand these changes so that you can eliminate as much of that anxiety as possible. The more accurate and detailed the information you have about your changing body, the more confident you will become about the adventure ahead. In this book you will learn about specific symptoms—what they mean and what you can do about them. You will also learn about personal reactions and feelings that may seem unusual to you. This book will help you to be well informed and confident so that your pregnancy will be as pleasant and safe as possible.

Modern medicine has made remarkable discoveries which have greatly reduced the discomforts and dangers which your great-grandmother faced. The years of medical research have greatly reduced the risks of pregnancy and have greatly increased the chances for a healthy normal childbirth.

But even though so much progress has been made in medical research, the March of Dimes, Birth Defects Foundation and Science Information Division still offer this caution: "Two to three percent of live births involve a significant congenital anomaly (abnormality) of some kind."

An abnormality in the number or structure of a chromosome can lead to a problem in the fetus. One such chromosomal abnormality is Down Syndrome, a condition commonly associated with a severe mental handicap.

In Down Syndrome the fetus has an extra chromosome 21. This is known as Trisomy 21 because the fetus has three copies of the chromosome 21 instead of two.

New information

A report issued in January 2003 by the American College of Obstetricians and Gynecologists and co-authored by the American Academy of Pediatrics concluded that the majority of brain injury cases in newborns do NOT occur during labor and delivery. Most instances of neurologic abnormalities occur prior to labor and birth. A task force formed in 1999 and comprised of experts from multiple specialties, issued a 94-page report confirming that most brain injury cases are not due to events that occur during labor, delivery, resuscitation, or treatment immediately following birth. For example, cerebral palsy and encephalopathy (brain injury) in many cases are due to events occurring before labor begins. The condition could originate from developmental or metabolic abnormalities, auto-immune or coagulation defects, infection, trauma, or a combination of these factors.

This report was endorsed not only by the National Institute of Child Health and Human Development of the National Institutes of Health, and the Centers for Disease Control and Prevention, both world renowned government health institutions, but also by distinguished non-government health organizations such as the March of Dimes Birth Defects Foundation, the Society for Maternal and Fetal Medicine, and the Child Neurology Society. International endorsements were given by the Australian and New Zealand Obstetricians and Gynaecologists, and the Society of Obstetricians and Gynaecologists of Canada.

While your clinician is helping you, however, there are many things you must do to cooperate. Your observations and questions are important to your healthcare provider who understands your desire to be completely informed about the changes occurring in your body.

It will be very helpful to keep this book handy in the months ahead. Between visits to your clinician during your pregnancy you will have questions about the way you feel. In this book you will find the answers to many of your questions and will probably find information you may not have even thought about so far.

What your clinician must know

Quality prenatal care is essential to your health and the future health of your child.

Studies indicate that poor prenatal care affects a person's intelligence. This implies that the in-utero environment has a strong effect on IQ in the general population.

Your clinician will be your main source of information and guidance throughout your pregnancy. Remember, you are working together to achieve the best care possible for you and your baby. Your intelligent observations and the information you give to him or her are important.

He or she will need to know basic facts such as your age, your weight, and whether you have been pregnant before. You'll be asked about your own family and the father's family. Is there any family history of chronic diseases such as high blood pressure, diabetes, heart or kidney diseases or allergies, including allergies to drugs? Have you ever had mumps, chickenpox, measles, hepatitis, or any previous operations?

There will be a physical exam and you will need to provide urine and blood samples. Your clinician may also request a Pap test.

Your blood test is important for several reasons. First, your baby receives its oxygen from hemoglobin in your red blood cells. If laboratory tests show that your hemoglobin is low (anemia) then your provider may consider supplements that will help maintain your energy and optimize nutrients transferred to the baby. The blood test will also show whether you are immune to Rubella (German measles) or are Rh negative (see pages 45-47).

You should objectively try to describe your working conditions and any potential stress that exists at work or at home. Menstrual cycles may go awry when a women experiences deep emotional stress or unusual physical demands. Occasionally a woman may be pregnant and still have some bleeding. So any previous irregularity in your menstrual cycle will be important for your healthcare provider to know.

There are also additional facts your clinician will be looking for. Let's review some of those to understand why they are important.

For example, you will need to recall the exact date of your last menstrual period. This date will help your clinician to decide approximately when your baby will be born. Here is a simple formula for determining the date your baby is due: count back 3 months from the first day of your last period and then add 7 days. So, if your last period began on August 1, then you can count backwards 3 months to May 1 and then add 7 days. Thus, your baby's due date is May 8th. This formula is based on studies which show that the baby will be born approximately 280 days after the last menstrual period.

Pregnancy is divided into three trimesters. Each trimester is approximately thirteen weeks. An average pregnancy lasts 280 days or forty weeks. It is more accurate to calculate the gestational age of the fetus in weeks than in months.

However, it's important to keep in mind that nature does not always cooperate with our formulas! Most babies arrive within a week of the calculated due date, few babies arrive exactly on the due date. It is perfectly normal for your baby's birth to occur within 1 to 2 weeks of the expected date.

Hepatitis B Screening (HBV)

The hepatitis B virus is the major cause of acute and chronic hepatitis and cirrhosis of the liver. If the mother carries this virus or has one of these diseases, the baby can become infected. Clinicians need to know this early in the pregnancy so that the baby can be vaccinated within 12 hours of delivery. According to a study by the American College of Obstetricians and Gynecologists (ACOG) in September of 1986, certain women are in high-risk groups for this virus and should undergo prenatal screening. The following is a list of the main high-risk groups, though there may be others:

- Women of Asian, Pacific Island, or Alaskan Eskimo descent, whether immigrant or United States born
- Women born in Haiti or sub-Saharan Africa
- Women with histories of:
  - Acute or chronic liver disease
  - Work or treatment in a hemodialysis unit
  - Work or residence in an institution for the mentally retarded

- Rejection as a blood donor
- Blood transfusion on repeated occasions
- Frequent occupational exposure to blood in medical or dental settings
- Household contact with an HBV carrier or hemodialysis patient
- Multiple episodes of sexually transmitted diseases
- Percutaneous use of illicit drugs (by injection)

Because accurate medical histories are often difficult to obtain, some clinicians routinely screen all their pregnant patients for hepatitis B. In an article appearing in the May 1999 journal, *Contemporary OB-GYN,* it was found that 90 percent of infants infected with hepatitis B became carriers of the disease. It is estimated that 20,000 infants are born to mothers who tested positive for hepatitis B in the United States. Safe and effective vaccines are available to prevent the fetus from becoming infected with this virus. If all pregnant women were tested for hepatitis B at one of their early prenatal visits, babies could be given hepatitis B immune globulin and the hepatitis B virus (HBV) vaccine if the mother had tested positive. The Centers for Disease Control and Prevention (CDC) and the American College of Obstetricians and Gynecologists (ACOG) now recommend that screening for hepatitis B be added to the routine prenatal testing procedures. Hepatitis B is transmitted through sexual contact, intravenous drug use or via blood transfusion.

Hepatitis A is spread by person-to-person contact or by exposure to contaminated food or water. The virus that causes hepatitis A is rare in pregnancy. Hepatitis A is not passed on to the fetus. If you should be exposed to hepatitis A during your pregnancy you should take immune globulin within two weeks of exposure.

Hepatitis C is transmitted through sexual contact, intravenous drug use and blood transfusions. Only a small percentage (less than 10 percent) of women testing positive for hepatiti C pass the infection to their baby. A woman testing positive for hepatitis C should not breastfeed her baby.

Sexually transmitted disease (STD)

According to the Centers for Disease Control and Prevention, sexually transmitted diseases have been linked to a marked increase in the number of ectopic pregnancies and infertility.

At a recent conference sponsored by Baylor College of Medicine in Texas, a professor and chairman of obstetrics and gynecology from Rush Medical College in Chicago recommended that every woman be tested during her first prenatal visit for the two most common STDs, gonorrhea and chlamydia.

Gonorrhea, if left untreated in the mother, may attack the eyes of a newborn as it travels through the birth canal. This is why antibiotic ointment or eye drops are placed in almost all newborns' eyes, to prevent blind-ness caused by a gonorrheal infection. Gonorrhea, like syphilis, can be treated and cured in most cases, thus helping to prevent complications compromising the health of the newborn.

Chlamydia is another sexually transmitted disease that is very prevalent today, particularly in younger women. It too can cause eye infections in the newborn as well as other illnesses such as pneumonia. Most clinicians now test for chlamydia on the first prenatal visit and again in the third trimester. Chlamydia can be treated with antibiotics but you must consult with your clinician who is aware of your pregnancy, to determine which, if any, antibiotic to take during your pregnancy.

Syphilis, in almost all cases, is spread through sexual activity with an infected partner or a carrier of the disease. Occasionally it can be transmitted by kissing if there is an open sore in the mouth of the infected person. An infected mother can also pass the disease on to her child. One of the problems with syphilis is that you may be unaware that you have the disease because symptoms may take years to surface. A blood sample is taken to test for syphilis.

But even if you have no symptoms, the disease can still be very dangerous, even deadly, to your baby. In the middle trimester of a pregnancy, the disease can pass through the placenta to the fetus. Consequences include structural birth abnormalities and possibly death of the developing baby. However, treating the infected mother for the disease can also help the child, and if the treatment is started early enough, chances are good for a healthy baby free of the disease.

Genital herpes is caused by a virus called herpes simplex and is transmitted by direct contact during sexual activity. An active infection is characterized by blisters and open sores primarily around the sex organs. Genital herpes may be associated with miscarriage as well as potential physical and mental disabilities.

It is important to tell your clinician if you have ever had genital herpes or had sexual contact with anyone who had the disease. Although not common, it is possible for a baby to become infected with the virus during a vaginal birth.

Should you show signs of an active herpes infection at the time of labor, a decision may be made to deliver your baby by cesarean section.

Acquired Immune Deficiency Syndrome and Human Immune Deficiency

Nearly everyone knows about the deadly disease called AIDS (Acquired Immune Deficiency Syndrome). Both (AIDS) and human immune deficiency are caused by the HIV virus. Once this virus gets into the blood stream it destroys the cells of the immune system. The immune system is the body's natural defense against infection. Thus, it is very important that you tell your clinician whether you or the father have AIDS, or test positive for HIV—not only for your own health and treatment but also because it is possible for the fetus to develop this disease.

HIV infected women who are pregnant, including those who have no symptoms of AIDS, treated with medications against the HIV virus are much less likely to pass the AIDS virus on to the fetus. The drug should be given to the HIV positive woman during her pregnancy, labor and delivery, and the baby must take the drug during the first six weeks of life. There is a test called enzyme-linked immunosorbent assay (ELISA) available to detect if your blood contains HIV antibodies—a sign of infection. The American College of Obstetrics and Gynecologists (ACOG) is now recommending that HIV screening be included in the standard series of tests for pregnant women— not just for women considered at high risk for this disease. Some states require that all pregnant women be tested for HIV.

The Food and Drug Administration (FDA) has cleared for market use the first oral, fluid-based, rapid HIV test with results available within 20 minutes.

Breastfeeding is not recommended for a baby whose mother is HIV positive since the baby could acquire HIV in this way.

Human papilloma virus (HPV), (also known as genital warts or condyloma) is another STD. It affects the genital area and is easily passed from one person to another during sexual intercourse, or oral or anal sex. Treatment of HPV can sometimes begin during pregnancy. However, if the warts are extensive, your doctor may want to wait until after your pregnancy to begin treatment.

The Physical Examination

It is essential for your clinician to perform a complete physical examination early in your pregnancy. The examination is routine and takes only a few minutes. Before the exam it is wise to empty your bladder and, if possible, have a bowel movement.

You will be asked to undress and to lie on the examination table with your heels in metal holders resembling stirrups on a horse's saddle. A sheet will be draped over the lower part of your body during the examination. If you have never had a vaginal examination, you may be surprised to learn that the clinician can actually feel where your uterus and ovaries are, and can tell if they are normal or enlarged. The physician can also determine if there is a possibility of a fibroid tumor or other obstacle which might hinder the growth of a fetus.

Try to relax. Breathing deeply through your mouth may help. With your legs separated, your clinician will insert two gloved fingers into the vagina while at the same time pressing lightly on your abdomen. By doing this, he or she can determine whether there are internal changes that are symptomatic of pregnancy. Such changes include a softening of the cervix and uterus as well as a bluish appearance to the cervix, vagina, and vulva. Shortly after conception, the uterus, cervix, and vagina begin to retain fluid. The resulting congestion and dilation of the veins in the area cause a dusky, blue appearance, clues that a pregnancy may be under way.

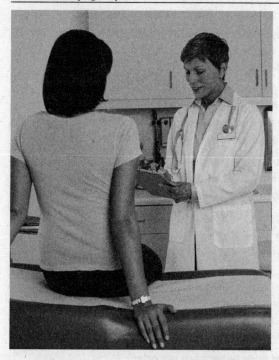

The condition of your breasts may also reveal symptoms of pregnancy. During pregnancy they become slightly tender to the touch and fuller. The nipples and areolas, the dark area around the nipples, become dark and slightly puffy.

Knowledge of your general physical condition is important to your clinician, particularly when you are pregnant. Using a stethoscope, the clinician will listen to your heartbeat and your breathing.

He or she may also place a stethoscope on your abdomen. Sometimes, but not always, the heartbeat of the fetus may be heard during the early months.

Fetal heart tones can be heard with the use of a stethoscope at 18-20 weeks gestation. It can be heard at 12 weeks with the use of an electronic stethoscope (doppler) that converts sound waves into signals you can hear.

Despite his or her experience in diagnosing pregnancies by a physical exam, there may be occasions when your clinician cannot be absolutely certain that you are pregnant. In such instances he/she may recommend a pregnancy test. There may be other instances when an ultrasound examination is performed to confirm the results of a pregnancy test.

Pregnancy tests

Pregnancy today, can be confirmed shortly after one missed period. No longer is it necessary to wait until you have missed two periods before going to your clinician for confirmation

One test for pregnancy uses a hormone in the woman's urine called human chorionic gonadotropin (hCG). This hormone is produced by the developing placenta and is excreted in the urine. Using an early morning urine sample, a clinician can determine pregnancy about a week after a missed period.

None of these tests will replace the physical exam, and your clinician may recommend various combinations of these tests, or perhaps some others. Whatever test you use, be sure to consult with your clinician as soon as you feel you are pregnant.

Home pregnancy tests

Pregnancy tests done in the home are considered by many to be as accurate as laboratory tests. These home tests use urine samples that are combined with a chemical to determine if a certain pregnancy hormone is present. Such tests are private, convenient, and inexpensive (though so are many laboratory tests). If the home test indicates you are pregnant, you should make an appointment to see your clinician as soon as possible.

Following the advice of your healthcare provider

When your examination is completed, your clinician will explain the findings. Once he/she is certain you are pregnant, you will be given instructions to follow during your pregnancy.

These instructions will vary slightly depending on your clinician. They will focus mainly on healthy eating and lifestyle to ensure you get proper nutrition and rest. It will also include things you should avoid such as alcohol, smoking and certain medications. He/she will likely discuss any changes you may need to make in your home and workplace.

As mentioned earlier, prenatal care is important for your health and your baby. Regular office visits with your clinician will be scheduled usually every four weeks during the first seven months, then more frequently after that.

You can find additional information throughout this book, but keep in mind there is no substitution for your clinician's advice. During your pregnancy you'll find many well-meaning friends and relatives anxious to tell you about their road to motherhood. Remember, their free advice is worth exactly what it costs—nothing!

Breast self-examination

It is very important that you continue doing breast self-examination every month throughout pregnancy, while nursing and thereafter.

About 2 percent of all breast cancers are diagnosed during pregnancy. Breast examination should be part of the prenatal visit and appropriate diagnostic tests should be performed if any abnormality is found, according to the American College of Obstetricians and Gynecologists (ACOG). This includes fine needle aspiration, ultrasound, open biopsy under local anesthesia and, in selected cases, mammography with proper shielding of the fetus. According to the American College of Radiology, no single diagnostic X-ray procedure results in radiation exposure to the extent that it is a threat to the well-being of the developing embryo or fetus. Therefore, exposure to X-ray during pregnancy is "not an indication for therapeutic abortion." However, because a woman's breasts during pregnancy are so dense, it is almost impossible to screen the breasts visually, making diagnostic imaging an unreliable method of finding or evaluating breast cancer during pregnancy. Prompt diagnosis and appropriate treatment are as essential in the pregnant woman as in the non-pregnant woman.

For more information on breast self-examination read, *A Guide to Breast Health Care—How to Examine Your Breasts,* also published by Budlong Press Company and available through your physician.

Chapter 2 What is happening

*M*UCH OF THE ANTICIPATION and excitement of your pregnancy over the next few months includes knowing how the process began and understanding what is happening to you and the new life you've created. Throughout the page of this book you'll see how much science has to share with you about this remarkable feat.

Each new human being grows from just two tiny cells, a female egg, called an ovum, and a male sperm. The female usually produces only one ovum each month. The egg, or ovum, is only ripe for a very short period of time. This is usually midway between menstrual periods. Though barely visible to the naked eye, it is one of the larger cells in the human body.

The male produces millions of tiny sperm that are among the smallest cells in the body. In fact, it takes many thousands of sperm to equal the ovum in size.

Each healthy sperm, has a minute whip like tail making it an extremely active, agile cell. During intercourse, millions of sperm are deposited in the vagina. The sperm, which can remain fertile for about 72 hours, swim up the vagina into the uterus and then into the fallopian tube searching for a ripe egg. When a fertile sperm reaches a ripe egg it penetrates the surface. The sperm sheds its tail and in an instant conception occurs.

Certainly not every act of intercourse will result in pregnancy. If the ovum is not fertilized during the short time it is ripe, the lining of the uterus breaks down and is expelled during menstruation. Even when pregnancy does occur, a baby will not always be born if either the sperm or ovum is defective. Nature frequently disrupts the pregnancy, ending it in a miscarriage. This is nature's way of helping ensure the survival of healthy future generations.

The role of the uterus

The uterus is truly remarkable. It is a hollow, pear-shaped organ located in the lower abdomen, weighing approximately 2 ounces and maintained at a constant temperature. The uterus serves as a "home" for the fetus for 9 months — allowing ample room for the fetus to grow without interfering with other organs in the region. A fallopian tube and one ovary extend from each side of the uterus, much like the branches of a tree.

The lower, narrower end of the uterus, sometimes referred to as the "neck" of the uterus, is the cervical canal (the birth canal during a vaginal delivery) which extends into the tube-like structure called the vagina.

Each of these organs plays its vital role in the reproductive process. As described previously, the healthy ovum and sperm, once united in the fallopian tube, then move, through the tube into the uterus. The united cells, now an embryo, become implanted in the prepared lining of the uterus. During the first eight weeks after conception the developing baby is called an embryo. After eight weeks it is referred to as a fetus.

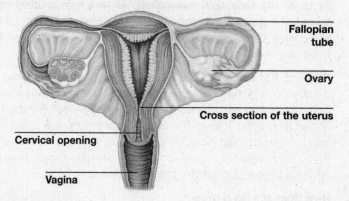

Fallopian tube

Ovary

Cross section of the uterus

Cervical opening

Vagina

Nourishment for the fetus

The uterus does much more than house your fetus for nine months. At conception, the embryo begins producing small active cells called "throphoblasts" that are attached to the lining of the uterus (endometrium). These cells seek out food for the embryo.

The placenta (afterbirth) begins to form by the time the embryo is 2 weeks old. Substances such as oxygen, nutrients, drugs, hormones, alcohol and almost everything else passes from the mother to the fetus through this semipermeable membrane. This route from the mother to the fetus also serves as a channel to remove all waste products from the fetus via the fetal vessels of the umbilical cord, to be excreted or disposed of by the mother's body. The placenta grows until it reaches its maximum size about 2 months before delivery. At this time it is about 8 to 9 inches in diameter. At birth the placenta weighs about 1 to 2 pounds.

Another process occurring within the uterus is the formation of amniotic fluid, which is contained in the "amniotic bag" (membrane) around the embryo. This amniotic fluid has several purposes. It provides a cushion against injury for the embryo; it gives the embryo some fluid; it keeps the temperature at a constant level; and it provides a liquid in which the embryo can move about.

Umbilical cord

As the embryo grows into the form of a baby, an umbilical cord grows from its navel. This long, semi-transparent, jelly-like rope is attached to the placenta and transports nourishment. The umbilical cord is really a continuation of the fetus' blood vessels. When the baby is born, it has served its function in the uterus and the cord is cut.

Research has found that blood from the umbilical cord contains the same disease fighting stem cells as are found in bone marrow. Unless you specifically request your baby's cord blood to be "banked" (saved) it will be discarded after birth. State-of-the-art procedures for preservation of these cells indicate they can last indefinitely. Private cord banks are available for a fee. If you are interested in this service you should consult your physician in advance of your due date for more information.

How does the fetus grow?

By the time you suspect you are pregnant, three or four weeks have typically passed since conception. Many changes have already taken place in your body. At five weeks (about three weeks after you missed your first period) your future child is still an embryo. This embryo is about 1 inch long, already has a two-lobed brain, a spinal cord, and a heartbeat still too faint to hear.

It is during the first trimester, from 2 to 8 weeks after conception, that the embryo is most vulnerable to the potential causes of birth defects.

By the end of the eighth week all major organs and systems are in place but not yet fully developed. The beginnings of the facial features, as well as the fingers, toes, ears, and eyes have begun to form.

The illustrations on pages 16 to 18 describe the growth of the fetus over the course of your pregnancy.

Fetal growth is affected by a number of factors including:
- Smoking which can reduce birth weight
- Illicit drug use which can slow fetal growth
- Multiple pregnancy, babies usually smaller
- Diabetes in the mother that can result in larger or smaller baby

Full-term babies, carried in the uterus through the nine months, measure 19 to 21 inches. The average weight for a girl is 7 pounds, a boy 7 1/2 pounds, although many babies may weigh as little as 5 1/2 to 6 pounds.

A baby born before 37 weeks is considered preterm. Preterm babies are at an increased risk for breathing problems, infections and other complications. Although medical science today has improved the survival rate of these smaller infants, preterm birth continues to be one of the most important problems of pregnancy.

Remember that all these figures represent averages. Even the time your clinician estimates you will carry your baby is based on an average. Barely one pregnancy in ten, results in a birth exactly 280 days after the beginning of the last menstrual period. Certainly no two children develop at the same rate after they are born, and the same holds true in the prenatal stage. So, if for example, you are given a due date of April 25th, it means your baby may be born shortly before or after that date.

Near the end of pregnancy, the cervix "ripens" that is, it thins out, softens, and may start to dilate. The term for this is effacement. When these changes occur before labor, it usually indicates that labor will be easier. If not, progress will be much slower. You should not be too concerned if you go past your expected due date by a week or possibly two – your provider will be following you very closely.

At 5 weeks the embryo is about 1 inch long and weighs less than an ounce. It has a two-lobed brain and a spinal cord. Tiny limb buds begin to appear which will eventually grow into arms and legs. The heart also forms, and though it is too faint to hear, it begins to beat on the 25th day.

At 8 weeks the embryo is 1 inch long and still weighs less than an ounce. All major organs and systems are formed but not yet fully developed. By the end of the second month of a pregnancy, the embryo is called a fetus.

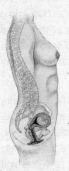

By the end of 3 months the fetus is 4 inches long and weighs just over one ounce. Buds for future teeth, soft finger and toenails, and hair appear on the fetus' head. The kidneys begin to secrete urine and there is further development of organs. An electronic stethoscope (doppler) can detect a heartbeat. From this time on the fetus begins to gain weight.

In the 4th month the fetus grows to 6 to 7 inches long and weighs about 5 ounces. Its own sex is developing. The fetus moves, kicks, sleeps, swallows, can hear and pass urine. The skin is pink and transparent and eyebrows have formed.

At 5 months the fetus will have a spurt in growth. The internal organs continue to mature. The fetus is much more active—turning from side to side and even flipping over. This is the month when movement is usually first felt by the mother. A stethoscope can detect a heartbeat. By the end of this month the fetus has grown and is 8 to 12 inches long and weighs from 1/2 to 1 pound.

In the 6th month the fetus continues to grow rapidly. There is continued development of organ systems. The skin is red, wrinkled and covered with fine hair. By the end of this month, the fetus will weigh 1 to 1 1/2 pounds and be 11 to 14 inches long. The lungs are still not fully developed and as a rule the fetus cannot live outside the uterus without specialized, high-tech support systems.

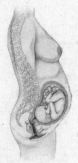

The 7th month is another rapid growth period. The fetus sucks its thumb, the eyes open and close, and fetal bones are hardening. The fetus now weighs about 3 pounds and is approximately 15 inches long. It now has a better chance of surviving if it is born.

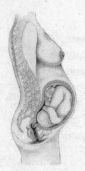

The 8th month shows continuing growth in the size and weight of the fetus. Though there is less room to move about, the kicks are felt more strongly. The fetus is now about 18 inches long and weighs about 5 pounds.

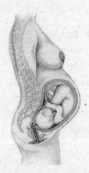

During the 9th month the fetus gains about 1/2 pound a week. The bones in its head are soft and flexible for delivery. Usually the fetus turns so as to settle into the optimal position for delivery. The fetus is considered full term, weighing between 6 and 9 pounds with an average length of 19 to 21 inches.

Ⅶ ITH ALL THE ACTIVITY GOING ON INSIDE YOUR BODY as your baby develops you may be wondering what other changes you should expect during your pregnancy. You already know your menstrual period will stop for nine months then resume after the baby is born. But what else can you expect both physically and emotionally?

Changes in your breasts

Your breasts are designed to produce milk to nourish the baby. Your body began preparing for this as soon as conception occurred. One of the first changes you will notice is your breasts will become larger, firmer, and more tender. Early in your pregnancy you may experience a tingling, pricking sensation near the nipples and extending outward.

The pinkish area around the nipple, called the areola, will become darker and you will notice small "bumps" appearing which are a part of the milk-producing glands. About your fourth month your breasts may exude a small amount of moisture. This fluid is called "colostrum" and is a forerunner to the future milk supply. Later on, enough colostrum may be secreted to necessitate placing an absorbent material over the nipples inside your bra to absorb leakage. Be sure to gently wash away the dried substance with warm water so your nipples won't become itchy, sore, or irritated. Do not use soap. This can cause dryness and irritation.

The veins in your breasts will probably become noticeably prominent. This is nothing to be alarmed about. They are simply working harder to carry a richer blood supply to help prepare your breasts for nourishing your baby.

Nausea

There are many hormonal changes taking place at this time and some, but by no means all, pregnant women complain of nausea during the first trimester of their pregnancy. Some may experience nausea only occasionally. Others report feeling waves of nausea for a short time early in the morning. Though it is commonly referred to as "morning sickness' it can occur at any time of the day. It may be worse among those who are excitable or have sensitive digestive systems. Usually this is only a temporary condition that disappears after the third month.

There are a few simple steps you can take to relieve the nausea and increase your comfort. Eat small, simple, frequent meals. Avoid fried and greasy foods. Cabbage, cauliflower, and spinach, which are hard to digest, should also be avoided. Do not avoid eating—this will make any nausea worse. If you have problems in the morning, try eating a dry diet such as a few crackers or dry toast. Stay in bed for 15 or 20 minutes, and rise slowly. You should then be able to have a normal breakfast in half an hour. At other times during the day, simply lying down for a few minutes can help. Other women find that nausea can be prevented if they lie down for 15 minutes after each meal. Acupressure, motion sickness bands and ginger have also been suggested as alternative treatments for nausea. Check with your healthcare professional before taking ginger or any anti-nausea medication.

If you are less than 6 weeks pregnant, you can take a folic acid supplement rather than your multivitamin containing folic acid since folic acid alone is less likely to upset your stomach and it is very important that you have sufficient folic acid early in your pregnancy

Frequent urination

As the uterus, the organ that is now home to your fetus begins to grow, it exerts pressure on the bladder. The pressure is the same as if the bladder were full. The result will be a more frequent need to urinate. Like nausea, this condition should clear up in a few weeks. Though it may return at the end of your pregnancy when the much larger fetus is being carried in the lower abdomen and again exerting pressure.

Another problem you may experience is leaking urine when you cough, laugh or sneeze. This is called stress urinary incontinence. As the uterus grows it puts pressure on the bladder. In addition, the relaxation of the pelvic floor muscles compound the problem particularly during the second and third trimesters. Kegel exercises (see pages 86 and 89) will help strengthen the pelvic floor muscles. If the urine leakage continues after delivery, continue with the Kegel exercises.

Despite this condition, do not cut back on your fluid intake, since fluids are very important to the growth of your baby. Clinicians recommend drinking a minimum of two quarts of liquids a day. Avoid taking any liquids for a couple of hours before going to bed to prevent interrupting your sleep.

Expanding waistline

By the beginning of the fourth month, the fetus may weigh five ounces and have grown to over six inches in length. It is encased in a fluid in the uterus and the walls of this elastic organ grow thicker to contain this extra load. These changes will cause your abdomen to distend. As it does, the skin will have to stretch and you may notice stretch marks—pink horizontal lines appearing on your abdomen. Some people may suggest putting rubbing lotion, cold cream, or oil on these marks. The truth is, there's not much you can do about them. You are either born to get them or not.

Keep in mind the importance of proper nutrition for you and your baby. Pregnancy is not the time to begin dieting. Follow your clinician's advice regarding your weight and refer to Chapter 6 for suggestions about nutrition and diet.

Feeling life

One of the most thrilling changes you will experience may occur about halfway through your pregnancy when you feel a faint, gentle fluttering in your abdomen. This is referred to as "quickening". You may not feel it again for several days. Then the movement will become more distinct. It will grow stronger and become more vigorous each day. In fact, toward the end of your pregnancy you will sometimes be able to stand before a mirror and watch the fetus' limbs press against the walls of your abdomen.

Clinicians are aware that even embryos move, although women can't feel them because the uterus is so well insulated. For this reason, some women miss that early fluttering though soon the movements are so strong as not to be mistaken for anything but fetal movement. What's happening? The fetus is likely stretching, moving its arms and legs and turning its head from side to side. But remember, a fetus won't move continuously. Sometimes it's asleep. Perhaps the biggest surprise is that fetuses move about as much as they do in the confined space provided for them.

If you have not felt the fetus moving at all by twenty-two weeks let your healthcare provider know. He or she may want to do an ultrasound. Sometimes the placenta is positioned on the front wall of the uterus and acts as cushion, delaying the time when movement is first felt. If you have been feeling life and notice the number of fetal movements has reduced or you do not feel any movement for several hours, lie down on your left side and drink something sweet such as juice or soda. If you do not feel at least ten movements within the next two hours call your clinician. Depending on how far along you are in your pregnancy they may want to perform further tests.

Contractions

Irregular contractions which can occur any time after the first trimester are known as Braxton Hicks contractions, named for the clinician who first described them.

For some women these are like menstrual cramps. They may occur more often toward the end of the pregnancy and are the cause of "false labor" — irregular contractions without the dilation of the cervix.

Emotional changes

There will likely be a number of questions you will have about the dramatic changes about to occur in your life. You may experience anxieties you never want to mention, especially if this is your first baby. If you relax and look at each concern logically you'll find it much easier to overcome your apprehension.

For example, you may worry about whether your baby will be born normal and healthy. The fact is that modern medicine has greatly reduced the risk of having an abnormal child. Sixty years ago, the infant mortality rates in the U.S. and Canada were 100 deaths for every 1,000 births. Today, that statistic has been reduced to 8.5 deaths per 1,000 births. When you start to worry about a malformed child, remember that modern medicine has put statistics on your side for having a healthy baby. Don't let worry be a problem itself.

You may also be concerned about how a new human being will affect your relationship with your husband. Of course, there will be changes. Sexual activity is going to change somewhat in the next nine months. And as your pregnancy continues, you and your husband may become impatient for the pregnancy to end. This is perfectly normal. As adults, you can deal with this through tolerance, good will, common sense and open discussions.

Sometimes expectant parents have difficulty understanding their new roles. But the transition does not mean that you will go from being a young, active couple to old, inactive parents. The activities which you enjoyed before need not change very much or at all. In fact, one effect that your pregnancy may well have is to deepen the relationship between you and your mate.

Your love for each other may strengthen the bond between you as you focus your love on the new baby. This new focus in no way has to diminish the love you shared before the baby.

Finally, you need to remember that childbirth is no longer shrouded in mystery. It is a perfectly normal and natural function. There have been many myths about pregnancy. Most of them are silly. For example, if a pregnant woman attends a funeral, it will affect her baby; going to the zoo and viewing ugly animals can mark your child. Or, if you listen to good music while pregnant, your baby will have musical talent. These myths are so foolish they are almost comical. They have no basis in fact. Birthmarks are coincidental and genetic, and not caused by your baby looking at a baboon. There is no correlation between your thoughts and the fetus' development. The fetus does not know whether you are at a funeral or a supermarket. When you start to become worried or hear stories such as these, remember, that as a woman you were born to give birth to a new human being.

If your concerns and worries during pregnancy begin interfering with your daily life, speak with your healthcare professional. Help is available.

Chapter 4 Reporting to your clinician

THROUGHOUT YOUR PREGNANCY YOU WILL BE VISITING regularly with your clinician. These appointments are usually brief but they are very important. Use this time to ask about any concerns you have about your pregnancy or what to expect after the baby arrives. Keeping the lines of communication open between you and your clinician is one of the surest ways to guarantee a pleasant, comfortable pregnancy.

As discussed in the previous chapter, mood swings related to the hormonal changes taking place during pregnancy are not unusual. But sadness that doesn't seem to go away can be a warning sign of depression. There has been much publicity about postpartum depression or "baby blues" but little has been said about depression during pregnancy. It is estimated that more than one in ten mothers-to-be experience depression that doesn't go away.

It is normal to occasionally feel sad, but if you feel sad most of the time you must report this to your healthcare professional and ask for help. Pregnant women who experience depression may not take care of their health and this could affect the fetus. Sadness that lasts for at least two weeks and has more than one of the following symptoms are signs of depression:

- Feeling depressed or "down" most of the day, almost every day.
- Feeling guilty, hopeless or unworthy.
- Lacking interest in work or other activities.
- Thinking about death or suicide.
- Feeling very tired most of the time. Loss of energy.
- Sleeping more than usual or not being able to sleep at night.

- Eating much more than is normal and gaining weight, or loss of appetite and losing weight.
- Being unable to make decisions or pay attention.
- Experiencing aches and pains not relieved by any treatment.

Some studies have suggested that a mother's depression and anxiety can have a strong impact on the pregnancy and the baby.

Keep the clinician up to date on how you feel. This book presents answers to questions and situations asked most often by pregnant women. Yet there will be times when, as an individual, you present unique problems. This is a period when you and your clinician are working together you must discuss any problems that relate to your pregnancy whether physical or mental.

Remember, too, that your clinician's nurse is an excellent source of information and support. Don't hesitate to discuss your concerns with the nurse who is an experienced professional trained to help you and to answer questions.

Your routine office visits are an excellent opportunity to answer those questions. These visits usually range from once a month up to the 28th week, then every two weeks until the ninth month, and once a week during this last month. Of course special circumstances or conditions can alter this schedule. During each visit it is important to check your weight, blood pressure, urine and the position of the fetus and its size. Routine prenatal visits are not time consuming, but they are vital.

Preexisting problems

Pregnancy can be stressful even if no prior medical problems exist. There are some preexisting health problems that can affect your pregnancy just as your pregnancy can affect a preexisting medical condition. A pregnant woman with a preexisting health problem will be followed more closely and may undergo additional tests to monitor her pregnancy as well as the preexisting condition.

It cannot be emphasized enough that women with a preexisting medical problem, whether diabetes, asthma, seizures or other chronic health problem have their condition under control before they become pregnant.

Do not stop taking any medication prescribed for your health problem when you learn you are pregnant. Instead, notify your doctor as he or she may want to adjust the dosage or change your medication.

Asthma

Asthma is a chronic disease of the respiratory system that causes wheezing, difficult breathing and coughing. Asthma is unpredictable during pregnancy. In some pregnant women their asthma improves, while in others it becomes worse or remains unchanged.

Most medications for asthma are safe during pregnancy but always let your doctor(s) know what medication you are taking and that you are pregnant. Asthma could pose a problem if the fetus does not get sufficient oxygen. An asthmatic attack in the mother will lower the oxygen available to the fetus so it is very important to try and keep your asthma under control.

- First and foremost if you smoke, **STOP!**
- Do not allow anyone to smoke in your home and avoid places where there is a lot of smoking.
- Recognize environmental triggers and avoid them if at all possible. If animal dander is the offender, find another home for your pet.
- Keep your home as dust free and mold free as possible.
- Your clinician may recommend flu immunization after your first trimester if you will be pregnant during the flu season.
- Notify your clinician if your asthma becomes worse. Do not wait until it is a full-blown attack, if at all possible.
- Do not delay treatment of any early symptoms of infection or pending asthmatic attack — call your clinician promptly.
- Go to the emergency room if an acute asthma attack does not respond to the first medication tried.

Dizzy spells and fainting

It is not unusual in the first four months of pregnancy to occasionally feel dizzy or lightheaded. Usually, you can remedy this by lying down on your side. It is not a serious condition and will stop in time. If it persists, you should tell your healthcare provider.

Shortness of breath

By the end of your last month of pregnancy the fetus has grown large enough to press on the rib cage and interfere somewhat with your breathing. As a result you may be a little short of breath when you climb stairs or engage in certain activities. Try to move more slowly and practice deep chest breathing. If you have trouble sleeping, prop yourself up in a semi-sitting position with several pillows

Infection

It is important that you report any sign of infection to your clinician. Under no circumstances should you try to treat yourself. Some antibiotics can be hazardous to you and/or your fetus. Should you need to be treated for an infection, your doctor will know which drug is the safest for you to take.

Influenza

A study conducted by a group of physicians at Vanderbilt University School of Medicine in Nashville, Tennessee, recommended that all pregnant women who were beyond the first trimester of their pregnancies during the influenza season be given the flu vaccine as recommended by the Advisory Committee of Immunization Practices of the Centers for Disease Control and Prevention (CDC).

The CDC recommends that pregnant women who have medical conditions that increase their risk for complications from influenza, be vaccinated before the influenza season, regardless of the stage of pregnancy. Discuss this with your healthcare professional.

Lyme Disease

Lyme disease is caused by a bite from an infected tick. Once the infected tick bites you, a round sore appears with a small center, similar to a bull's eye. This infection can spread to the joints and cause arthritis, even after the round sore has disappeared. Doctors can usually cure Lyme disease with safe antibiotics. But if it is not treated, the infection may spread to your heart and nervous system. Research has also shown that the bacteria can pass from the infected mother to the fetus and cause birth defects or miscarriage. Because of the possible dangers of this disease, clinicians advise pregnant women to avoid heavily wooded areas, or if they have to be there, to wear long-sleeved shirts, slacks, and socks and to keep their hands and face protected.

The FDA has approved a blood test for Lyme disease. The test results are available in 20 minutes. A vaccine for Lyme disease was previously available; however, it has been withdrawn form the market.

Nosebleeds

During pregnancy, hormone levels increase. This change increases the amount of blood your body makes to meet the needs of the growing fetus. As a result of the increase in your hormone level the mucous membranes inside your nose may swell, become dry and therefore bleed easily. To relieve these symptoms:

- Increase your fluid intake.
- Use a humidifier to moisten the air in your house. Be sure the humidifier is cleaned daily.
- If you must, use saline nose drops to help open your nasal passage. Do not use any decongestants unless your healthcare professional specifically advises you to do so.

Heartburn

After eating it is not unusual to experience some stomach discomfort, gas or belching. You may even have a slight burning sensation in your chest. To help avoid or minimize heartburn you should:

- Avoid eating spicy and greasy foods.
- Take a tablespoon of cream before meals. This will coat your stomach lining and cause better activity in the intestines.
- Eat more slowly.
- Avoid lying flat, particularly after eating. An extra pillow at night may give you some relief.
- If heartburn persists, call your clinician.

Recently, doctors at the University of Alabama, Birmingham Medical Center reported that chewing gum can help and even prevent symptoms of heartburn. Their recommendation was to chew gum for about 30 minutes immediately after eating.

Constipation

When your uterus grows larger, it will press on your lower intestines and may cause constipation. You can help this condition by avoiding constipating foods such as cheese, chocolate and rice. Simple adjustments in your diet can help relieve this condition. You may find that fruit, especially at night, is a good laxative. Prunes, figs, peaches, and cherries are effective and also nourishing. Increasing the roughage in your diet will also help your bowel movements. Roughage is found in green vegetables, either cooked or raw, and whole grain bread. For breakfast, eat whole grain or bran cereals. Begin each morning by drinking a glass of water and continue with a total of 8 glasses of water or juice throughout the rest of the day.

If the problem persists, do not be embarrassed to tell your clinician.

Hemorrhoids

Constipation can also cause hemorrhoids, enlarged veins at the opening of the rectum. Eating fiber and roughage will soften the stool and make passage easier. Do not experiment on your own with over-the-counter drugs for this condition. Instead, tell your clinician. He or she may recommend a stool softener.

Muscle cramps

As your fetus grows larger, it may put pressure on the large blood vessels in your lower abdomen. This can slow up the blood circulation in your legs and cause cramps. To relieve the discomfort try putting a heating pad or hot water bottle under the cramped muscles. Gently massaging the legs may also bring relief, or try bending your foot upward with your hands. Wearing comfortable shoes with low heels can also help. Do not use liniment. It will not help. Sometimes, the baby's head can put pressure on some nerves and cause shooting pains in your legs. Try changing your position or doing a few minutes of knee-chest positioning. Before going to bed, try stretching your legs, this sometimes relieves leg cramps.

Pain extending from the lower back down to one or the other leg is called sciatica. It is due to pressure on the sciatic nerve. Heat applied to the painful areas can usually provide relief. If the pain is severe, contact your healthcare professional.

Varicose veins

Varicose veins occur during pregnancy when certain veins become weakened and enlarged due to the increased pressure from the growing uterus. These enlarged veins occur most frequently in the legs but may also appear in the region of the vulva and vagina. Varicose veins can be quite uncomfortable. You cannot completely prevent varicose veins, but you can stop the painful throb that accompanies them. Try not to stand or sit for long periods of time without moving. Keep the blood circulating by walking and moving. You can also elevate your legs when you are sitting down to help the blood flow back from your feet through the rest of your body more efficiently. Do not cross your legs when sitting and avoid wearing knee-highs or stockings with a tight elastic band. Support hose can provide comfort, especially if you put them on before you get out of bed

Your sleep

During the first few months of your pregnancy you may feel constantly tired—as though you can't seem to get enough sleep. If this is the case, try to organize your time so that you can work in a midday nap—or even a nap in the morning and another in the afternoon.

By the end of your pregnancy, however, it may be the inability to fall asleep (insomnia) that is most troubling. Your increased girth may require a change in sleep positions. Try using an extra pillow or two to prop yourself up in bed if you have difficulty falling asleep. Try taking a walk before bedtime. Other relaxing techniques include a warm bath or shower before retiring; even a warm glass of milk before bedtime can help you relax. Do not take any sedatives (sleeping pills) or tranquilizers.

Vaginal discharge

Even when you are not pregnant, your vagina secretes a small amount of liquid, though it is hardly noticeable. But when you become pregnant, this discharge may increase. Such an increase is caused by the changes in the vaginal cells that are becoming softer, thicker, and more elastic so that the baby can be born. Some seepage of fluid comes from the cervix. You really cannot stop this discharge, but you can keep the area clean by washing frequently with mild soap. However, do not douche. Tell your clinician if the discharge is excessive, if there is itching, or if you experience a sudden gush of water or constant leaking. (See PROM on page 39.)

Rubella (German measles)

Rubella is caused by a virus that is known to be a teratogen, a compound that can cause structural changes to a fetus during development. Rubella is a very dangerous disease for pregnant women and their babies. If you contract Rubella early in your pregnancy, your fetus can be severely damaged. The first 6 weeks are the most critical time, because the disease can then affect your fetus' heart, eyes, and ears, which develop in the second 6 weeks.

There is less possibility of damage the later in your pregnancy that you contract the disease. If your fetus' organs are already structurally sound, there is generally no damage. Here are some points to remember:

- If you have had German measles before, you will not get it again.
- The expectant mother must have German measles during pregnancy for the fetus to be affected. Exposure alone will not harm the fetus.
- If you have had contact with German measles and have not had the disease or are unsure if you have had the disease, call your clinician. He or she will arrange for you to come to the office in an off-hour so that you will not expose other pregnant patients.
- There are blood tests to determine whether you have had the disease in the past or have it now.
- Any woman who is given the Rubella vaccine should wait 28 days before becoming pregnant. If you get pregnant before this period of time has elapsed, ask your clinician for advice. Since abnormalities rarely occur from a vaccine exposure, termination of pregnancy is usually not advised.
- Pregnant women exposed to Rubella should seek counseling regarding the risk to their unborn child.

Varicella-zoster (Chickenpox)

Another childhood disease that can have serious consequences in adults and particularly in a pregnant woman, is chickenpox. Chickenpox is caused by the varicella-zoster virus and it can be transmitted across the placenta to the fetus. Women who contract chickenpox between the second and fourth months of their pregnancies, have been known to have a higher incidence of miscarriage or to deliver babies with congenital malformations. It therefore is imperative that pregnant women who have not already had chickenpox, avoid contact with anyone who has chickenpox or shingles, another form of the disease also caused by the varicella-zoster organism.

When chickenpox is contracted late in pregnancy the baby may be born with chickenpox or may be protected by the mother's antibodies. However, if the mother contracts the disease within a week of delivery there is not enough time for the antibodies to develop and cross the placenta to protect the fetus. In this situation the baby is more likely to become seriously ill or possibly die.

There is a drug called varicella-zoster immunoglobulin that can be given to a pregnant women who becomes infected, which may help prevent her from developing a severe form of the disease if it is given within 96 hours of exposure. It may not however, protect the fetus from infection.

There is now a vaccine for chickenpox which the American Academy of Pediatrics recommends be given routinely in early childhood, as well as for susceptible older children and adolescents. A single dose should be given between 12 and18 months of age. You will need to check with your pediatrician or family physician for any contraindications to this vaccine. However, this vaccine is NOT given during pregnancy.

Fifth Disease

The fifth disease, caused by the human parvovirus B19, is named because it was the fifth to be discovered among a group of diseases characterized by fever, rash and mild flu-like symptoms in children. Its adverse effect during pregnancy was first recognized in 1984. Though the disease is mild in children it is a cause for concern if a woman is exposed to the human parvovirus B19 during her first or early second trimester. Fifth disease is known to cross the placenta and infect the fetus, possibly causing sudden anemia, heart failure or other problems requiring treatment. It also increases the risk of a miscarriage. If you have been exposed to the human parvovirus B19, be sure to notify your clinician promptly.

Group B Streptococcus

Group B streptococcus (GBS) is a bacteria commonly found in the vagina or rectum of pregnant women. In most cases no symptoms or problems occur. A woman with GBS may pass this bacteria on to her baby during labor and delivery. Some babies exposed to GBS disease will become infected. The infection can occur early, within 7 days of birth with most such infections occurring during the first 6 hours. Early problems in the baby as a result of this disease may even result in death.

Risk factors for group B streptococcus are:

- Preterm labor (less than 37 weeks gestation)
- Preterm rupture of the membranes (less than 37 weeks gestation)
- Rupture of membranes 18 hours or longer
- Previous birth of a baby with GBS
- GBS bacteria in the urine during the current pregnancy
- Mother in labor with a fever of 100.4° F (38° C) or higher

The Centers for Disease Control and Prevention (CDC) guidelines now recommend all pregnant women, not just those with risk-based factors, be screened at 35 to 37 weeks gestation, for group B streptococcal (GBS) colonization in order to prevent early-onset GBS in newborns. Recent CDC data demonstrated that screening all pregnant women was over 50 percent more effective than screening only those with risk-based factors. They now recommend vaginal and rectal GBS cultures at 35-37 weeks gestation for all women

Treatment during pregnancy is indicated when:

- There was a previous infant with invasive GBS
- GBS bacteria is found in urine during the current pregnancy

- A positive GBS screening culture during current pregnancy (unless a C-section is planned)
- The GBS status is unknown and any of the following events occur:
  - Delivery at less than 37 weeks gestation
  - Membranes ruptured for 18 hours or more
  - A fever during pregnancy of 100.4° F (38°C) or higher

The development of a vaccine to prevent group B streptoccal disease in mothers and their infants is now in progress. The vaccine will contain the 5 types of GBS found in 98 percent of GBS infections in the United States.

Listeriosis and salmonella

Listeriosis and salmonella are two of the most common food-borne illness caused by bacteria. The bacteria responsible for causing listeriosis and salmonella food poisoning are often found in raw poultry, eggs, milk, fish and products containing these ingredients. Salmonella poisoning symptoms occur 24 hours after eating contaminated food. The most common symptoms are diarrhea, fever and abdominal pain that usually lasts from 2 to 4 days but may last longer. The symptoms may be more severe in pregnant women.

Listeriosis symptoms include the sudden onset of fever, headache, muscle cramps, abdominal pain, nausea, diarrhea, and vomiting. Sometimes there are no symptoms. The listeria bacteria can infect the fetus during pregnancy, causing a spontaneous abortion, stillbirth or an infected newborn. This is why this infection is of particular concern to pregnant women. Epidemic outbreaks of listeriosis have been associated with raw vegetables and dairy products, including unpasteurized milk and soft cheeses.

Public health experts warn pregnant women not to eat certain types of cheeses, such as goat cheese, Brie, Camembert, blue-veined or other soft cheeses. Hispanic women are particularly at risk because soft cheeses are used regularly in Latin American kitchens. Do not eat any cheese made from unpasteurized milk since it may contain the listeria bacteria which can cause miscarriage, infection or premature labor.

A pregnant woman with flu-like symptoms, back pain and premature labor should be tested for listeriosis, according to an article in the April 1999 issue of the *Contemporary OB/GYN Journal*. If the infection is diagnosed, the patient should be treated to prevent the infection from spreading to the fetus.

Lower abdominal pain

Bands of fibrous tissue which are the round ligaments on each side of the abdomen support the uterus. As the uterus grows, these bands are stretched. You may feel as if something is pulling in this area, or you may even have a sharp pain in the lower abdomen on one side or the other. The pain occurs most frequently between weeks 18 and 24 of the pregnancy. Avoiding rapid changes in position will help prevent these pains. If you should feel sharp pain in the groin area, try bending toward the side of the pain. If the abdominal pain persists or becomes more acute, call your clinician.

Miscarriage

Miscarriage occurs most frequently during the first three months of a pregnancy though it can occur any time during the first half of a pregnancy. As many as 20 percent of pregnancies end in a miscarriage. The fetus is unable to survive outside the mother's body at this stage of the pregnancy. In the microscopic examinations of embryos and fetuses after a miscarriage, it was found that more than 80 percent revealed an abnormality that would prevent a surviving baby from living a normal life. A miscarriage in many cases then, is one of nature's built-in checks to assure the survival of healthy future generations.

Vaginal bleeding is the most common symptom of a miscarriage. Spotting early in the pregnancy does not always mean a miscarriage, however. Sometimes at the beginning of a pregnancy when the fertilized egg first attaches itself to the lining (endometrium) of the uterus, spotting or staining can occur. This is called implantation. Should you notice any bloody discharge however, report it to your clinician immediately. He or she will probably prescribe bed rest.

Recurrent miscarriage is 2 or 3 pregnancy losses in a row within the first 15 weeks gestation. It is distinct from an isolated miscarriage. Women experiencing recurrent miscarriage should consult their physician for specific testing.

Incompetent Cervix

This describes a cervix which is unable to perform its required function of retaining a pregnancy, frequently resulting in miscarriage or preterm birth in the second trimester.

Cervical incompetence may be the result of previous cervical trauma due to surgery or a difficult vaginal delivery, or it may be due to a genetic malformation of the cervix. These factors make it more likely for a recurrence of this problem in subsequent pregnancies.

The primary symptom of an incompetent cervix in pregnancy is spotting or bleeding. The majority of miscarriages are due to an abnormality in the fetus (see page 35). However, recurrent miscarriages, that is, 3 or more in a row, may be due to an incompetent cervix. Fortunately, today, with the aid of ultrasound (see pages 53-55), indications of an incompetent cervix can be determined and treated early on. One such surgical treatment is called cerclage. In this procedure, 1 or 2 sutures encircling the cervical opening are placed. The purpose of the suture is to tighten the cervix to prevent it from dilating under the growing weight of the fetus. The suture is removed approximately 1 week before delivery.

Another treatment, a non-surgical approach, used alone or in conjunction with a cerclage, is the use of a pessary, which is precisely fitted to the individual patient. A number of different pessaries have been used during pregnancy.

With the aid of ultrasound, certain risk factors for premature labor can be identified early and treatment can begin prior to the onset of symptoms. Your clinician may also recommend bedrest and the administration of a tocolytic agent (used to stop labor) to relax the muscles of the uterus, if there are no contraindications for its use.

Ectopic pregnancy

As explained earlier, a fertilized egg implants itself in the lining of the uterus and develops into an embryo. But if the embryo attaches itself outside of the uterus (usually in a fallopian tube), this is known as an ectopic pregnancy, and such pregnancies do not survive.

Because an ectopic pregnancy is very dangerous, even life-threatening, you should be alert for the symptoms. Dizziness, paleness, light-headedness, sweating, and rapid pulse may indicate internal bleeding leading to shock. Low abdominal pains and light vaginal bleeding are other signs. Sometimes there is pain in the shoulders — this pain is caused by blood escaping from a rupture into the abdomen and putting pressure on the diaphragm (the partition between abdominal and chest cavities) and in turn on the shoulders.

Current treatment can include medical therapy and minimally invasive surgery. Once a woman has an ectopic pregnancy there is an increased chance of another occuring each time she becomes pregnant.

You should also be aware that smoking can affect ectopic pregnancies. Researchers in France discovered that women who smoke have a two-thirds greater risk of an ectopic pregnancy than do nonsmokers. If you smoke at least half a pack a day, the risk is double.

Preeclampsia (Toxemia)

If a patient develops high blood pressure combined with protein (albumin) in her urine for the first time during the second half of her pregnancy, it is called preeclampsia (formerly known as toxemia). This is why your blood pressure is taken and a urine sample tested at each office visit. About 7 percent of pregnant women develop preeclampsia.

Doctors do not know exactly what causes this condition. Signs of preeclampsia such as fluid retention (swelling of face, legs and hands) and headaches should be reported to your healthcare professional immediately. He or she will want to check your blood pressure and a urine sample. An elevated blood pressure and protein in the urine are symptoms of preeclampsia.

A study reported in the March 2002 issue of *OB-Gyn News,* found that women who were physically active during their first 20 weeks of pregnancy had a reduced risk for preeclampsia. This supports ACOG guidelines (see pages 85-89) recommending pregnant women engage in moderate exercise on most if not all days, unless there are specific contraindications.

Preeclampsia is most common in first pregnancies. It is also seen more frequently in women who have a history of high blood pressure, heart disease,

diabetes, have twins or triplets or other chronic disease prior to their pregnancies. Preeclampsia can develop rapidly at any time, and it is not self-limit-
ing. If left untreated, the condition can progress to include convulsions and
coma, known as eclampsia. But it can often be prevented or controlled if monitored carefully. This is why it is so important to have regular prenatal visits.

Urinary tract infections

While frequent urination is common during early and late pregnancy a severe
reduction in urination may be an indication of a kidney infection called
pyelonephritis.

Symptoms include chills, fever, back pain and possibly swelling and pain
in your legs. Pyelonephritis is a serious kidney infection always requiring
antibiotics, frequently administered intravenously. Pyelonephritis makes you
sick and uncomfortable. You must report the symptoms to your clinician
so he or she can provide the necessary treatment before it leads to further
complications.

Bladder infections (cystitis) are infections not involving the kidneys. Cystitis
is common in pregnancy and may cause symptoms such as frequent urination, burning sensation on urination and an almost constant urge to urinate
but only in very small quantities. Sometimes there are no symptoms and the
bladder infection is diagnosed from testing the urine specimen you brought
in. Cystitis is usually treated with oral antibiotics. Not taking the antibiotics
prescribed for your urinary tract infection (UTI) could increase the risk of a
kidney infection and the health risk to your baby.

It will be necessary to drink 8 to 10 glasses of water a day in order to flush
out the kidneys.

Placenta Previa and Abruptio Placentae

Heavy bleeding occurring in the second half of a pregnancy suggests a problem with the placenta. The two most common problems involving the placenta are placenta previa and abruptio placentae.

Placenta previa occurs when the placenta lies very low in the uterus partial-
ly or completely covering the cervix blocking the baby's exit from the uterus.

Normal Pregnancy

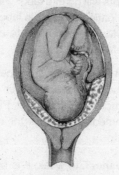

Placenta Previa

Abruptio Placentae

When the cervix dilates (begins to open), bleeding occurs requiring immediate medical attention.

Abruptio placentae is the result of the placenta detaching or separating from the uterine wall either before or during birth and is usually followed by heavy bleeding and constant and severe abdominal pain. The detachment and heavy bleeding may deprive the baby of oxygen.

Maternal cocaine use has been associated with a marked increase in the risk of abruptio placenta.

If you have any bleeding late in your pregnancy it is important that you notify your clinician immediately. Hospitalization for as long as several weeks may be necessary. Both placenta previa and abruptio placentae may require early delivery of the baby, usually by cesarean birth.

Premature Rupture of Membranes or PROM

The main symptom of premature rupture of membranes (PROM) is a sudden gush of water before the 37th week of pregnancy. What has happened is that the membrane or bag of water surrounding your fetus has ruptured (torn). PROM is the major cause of premature labor.

About half of preterm patients will go into labor within 24 hours of PROM and over 85 percent of preterm patients will be in labor within a week. If your clinician does diagnose PROM, you may have to be hospitalized so that you and your baby can be carefully monitored.

Other symptoms of PROM are increased vaginal discharge, menstrual-like cramps, backaches, and contractions, whether painful or painless. These symptoms are more common in women with PROM. If you notice any of these, call your clinician immediately, and in the meantime rest in bed.

Premature Labor

If your labor begins before the 37th week, it is called preterm or premature labor. A premature baby usually has more problems. Symptoms of premature labor include:

- Menstrual-like cramps which may be constant or intermittent (on and off)
- A feeling of heaviness or pressure on your rectum or perineum
- Lower back pain
- Cramps, with or without diarrhea
- Change in vaginal discharge (it may be heavier, watery or blood-tinged)
- Contractions

If you notice any of these signs, you should lie down on your side for an hour.

If the symptoms do not disappear, call your clinician and give him/her:

- Your name
- The date your baby is due
- Your symptoms
- The frequency of any contractions

Your clinician may take various actions. He or she may ask you to come to the office or go directly to the hospital. You may be given some drugs, called tocolytic agents to stop the labor. They can be given in IV fluids, by injection, or orally, and they work to relax the muscles of the uterus. Side effects may include nausea, vomiting, headache, tremors, flushing of the skin, and/or increased heartbeat.

Post Maturity (Post Term)

As explained earlier, your due date is approximate. You can deliver 2 weeks before or 2 weeks after that due date. Babies born after 42 weeks of gestation are called post mature, and they may have problems that babies delivered at term do not have. Recent evidence has prompted some physicians to consider 41 weeks as the time for additional testing or the induction of labor.

Cytomegalovirus

Modern science has identified this virus which can cross the placenta to the fetus and cause disease or impairment. The symptoms in the mother include fever, infection, sore throat and swollen glands. Sometimes there are no symptoms, and in non-pregnant, healthy adults, the virus may cause no problems even though it exists indefinitely in the body. Since not much is known about the virus or its treatment, it is best to try to prevent getting it.

Researchers suspect that it is spread through personal contact, so personal hygiene is essential. If you work in a day-care center or are around other babies, be careful to wash your hands after handling them or their diapers. The virus can be passed through urine or respiratory secretions.

So far, researchers believe that if a woman is infected with cytomegalovirus for the first time during pregnancy, her baby may be in danger. However, if the woman had been infected before she became pregnant and experiences a flare-up during pregnancy, the risk may not be as great for the fetus. The body produces antibodies during the original infection, and these antibodies protect both the mother and the fetus if there is a reinfection. Breastfeeding is another way that the virus can be passed from mother to baby. However, because the mother has passed antibodies to the virus across the placenta to the fetus, the fetus may not develop the infection. There may be a problem if the nursing mother acquires the virus after the baby is born. There may also be a problem if the baby is given pooled milk from a breast milk bank and one of the bank's donors transmitted the virus in her milk. If you know or suspect that you have been infected with this virus, tell your clinician.

If the baby has symptoms of this disease at birth it can result in jaundice (yellow pigmentation of the skin and whites of the eyes), microcephaly (a very small head), mental retardation, deafness and eye problems.

What to report to your clinician immediately

Over 90 percent of all pregnancies progress perfectly and are uneventful from a medical viewpoint. Most of the situations mentioned earlier are easily remedied, and their discomfort is only slight.

There are some symptoms though, which should be reported to your clinician as soon as they occur. Many of these can be treated before they progress to cause serious problems.

Should you develop any of the following symptoms do not wait until your next appointment to report them, but call your healthcare professional right away.

- Any sign of bloody discharge from the vagina.
- Persistent severe headaches.
- Severe nausea and vomiting. Occurring several times within an hour.
- Swelling of the face, ankles, feet, and hands, particularly if any of these puff up suddenly and your finger rings feel tight. (Slight swelling during last months in hot weather is customary.)
- Chills and fever of over 100° not accompanied by a common cold.
- Continued abdominal pains that are not relieved by a bowel movement.
- A sudden gush of water from the vagina.
- Frequency and burning on urination.
- An unusual increase in thirst, with reduced amount of urine. If you do not urinate for 12 hours even though you have had a normal intake of fluids report the condition immediately.
- Blurring of vision or spots before the eyes.

We mentioned earlier that your intelligent observations are important. Ask your healthcare provider which of these symptoms if any, deserve special attention in your case. Some of these may occur during normal pregnancy. For instance, abdominal pains could be due to something you ate. A sudden gush of water often precedes the beginning of labor. Unpleasant odors may make you dizzy and nauseated. However, sometimes these signs do precede the possibility of a miscarriage, preeclampsia, and/or urinary infections.

In this chapter we have tried to briefly cover most physical situations that may occur during pregnancy. Be assured that no one woman experiences every discomfort. Most rarely experience more than one or two. But being prepared to handle any situation intelligently will safeguard you and your baby and give you greater peace of mind.

Questions to ask my clinician

_____

_____

_____

_____

Phoning your clinician

About 4 A.M. one morning, Mrs. Brown stumbled back into bed, awoke her husband, and said, *"Call the clinician, I'm spotting."*

Mr. Brown hastily put on his robe, dialed the clinician's number, and the following conversation ensued:

"Hello, Dr. Greene speaking."

"Dr. Greene, this is Jim Brown. My wife is spotting."

Dr. Greene, awakened from a deep sleep, is desperately trying to determine which of the three Mrs. Browns in his practice it is. He asks, *"How much is she spotting?"*

"I don't know. I'll ask her. Just a moment."

The question is relayed from husband to wife. The answer is relayed from wife to husband to clinician, who is still not sure which Mrs. Brown is involved. The clinician's next question, *"When did I see your wife last?"* results in another round of relayed messages until finally the clinician believes he knows who the patient is.

Ongoing, accurate communication between you and your healthcare provider is extremely important during your pregnancy. This will make it easier to resolve any problems, or emergencies which might occur between office visits.

Except in extreme emergencies, you should be the only one speaking with your healthcare provider. Avoid relaying information to the clinician through your spouse or other family member.

Some simple procedures can help eliminate confusion:

1. Call during regular office hours whenever possible. With your records available at the office, it is easier for your clinician to manage your problems from there. Give information to the nurse. If it is a routine question, she may be able to give you an immediate answer, and she can always determine the necessity of your speaking directly to the clinician. If he/she can't come to the phone, she may relay the question or have the clinician return your call as soon as possible.

2. Any time you call, whether it is to the office during the day or directly to the clinician during non-office hours, give your full name, when you last saw the clinician, and your present month of pregnancy. Describe your situation in concrete terms. How much blood is being passed? How often? What does it look like? When did you last urinate? About how much? A cup? A teaspoonful? How much water did you drink since then? How often are your headaches? If there is swelling, where? For how long? Being specific can facilitate treatment.

3. Make the call yourself if at all possible. Relaying messages through a third party may give your clinician misleading information.

4. Always have a pencil and paper at the phone before you call. Write down whatever you are told to do. Making an emergency phone call when you are upset may cause you to misunderstand your clinician's instructions.

5. Know the name, address, and phone number of your pharmacy. Your clinician may need to contact them to prescribe a medicine.

6. At the beginning of your last month, you should ask your clinician when he or she wants to be called after labor begins.

Clinician's phone number: _____

Pharmacy's phone number: _____

Chapter 5 Tests during pregnancy

*T*HE MIRACLE OF BIRTH CONTINUES to inspire every generation. This inspiration is also evident with each generation of science as we see how far medicine has progressed with more sophisticated testing and information available to the mother during her pregnancy.

Even during the most normal pregnancy, an expectant mother will be tested and monitored on a regular basis. Prenatal care includes not only blood tests, but also routine urine analysis, measurement of weight gain and blood pressure readings. In addition to these, more sophisticated tests are being used to evaluate the health of both the mother and the fetus, particularly those considered to be at high-risk. The procedures available today are by no means necessary in every case, but if your clinician feels your situation warrants it, he or she may recommend certain tests.

Reasons for testing

There are a variety of reasons why a clinician may decide certain testing is advisable.

Rh Incompatibility

There are four blood types: A, B, AB, and O. These blood types are determined by the antigens in the blood cells. An antigen is a protein on the surface of blood cells. There are also minor antigens — the most common is called the Rh factor.

During your initial physical exam a routine blood test will determine your blood type and whether you are Rh positive or negative.

If the Rh factor is present you are Rh positive. If it is absent, you are Rh negative. Approximately 85 percent of Caucasians and a slightly higher percentage of African Americans and Asians, are Rh positive.

During pregnancy, it is normal for a small amount of the fetus' blood to mix with the mother's blood. If the mother is Rh negative and the father is Rh positive (as a large majority of people are), the fetus can acquire the Rh positive factor from the father. When this occurs, the fetus' blood differs from the mother's and the mother's blood can respond as if it were allergic to the fetus' blood by making antibodies to attack the Rh positive blood of the fetus.

This condition is called sensitization and it can cause serious problems. If the antibodies from the mother's blood cross the placenta into the fetus' blood, these antibodies will break down the red blood cells in the fetus, resulting in anemia. This is a very serious condition known as erythroblastosis fetalis, hemolytic disease or, more simply Rh disease. It can cause illness or even death to the fetus or newborn.

Fortunately, modern medicine can usually prevent the main cause of this disease, sensitization to the Rh factor. Once antibodies are formed, they never go away. The best course of action is to prevent the mother from becoming sensitized in the first place. If you have not been sensitized, your doctor may give you Rh immunoglobulin (Rhlg) or RhoGAM® near the 28th week of your pregnancy. If the baby is Rh-positive, you will be given another dose shortly after delivery. This treatment is to prevent you from developing antibodies to the Rh-positive cells from your baby that might have occurred during labor and/or delivery. This would avoid the risk to your fetus in any future pregnancies. Repeat doses of Rhlg are given with each pregnancy and birth of an Rh-positive baby. RhoGAM should also be administered following a miscarriage, abortion, ectopic pregnancy or other situations presenting a risk of the fetus's blood entering the bloodstream of the mother.

According to the American College of Obstetricians and Gynecologists, Rhlg is safe for pregnant women. The only two known side effects are a temporary soreness where the drug was injected and a slight fever.

Multiple births

During the fifth month when your baby's heartbeat pounds rhythmically, your clinician may detect more than the usual thumping indicating the possibility of two sets of heartbeats. If the clinician notes that your uterus is larger than normal for the number of months you are carrying, he or she may suggest an ultrasound test which provides an outline picture of the fetuses on a TV screen without the risk associated with X-rays.

How Rh disease develops

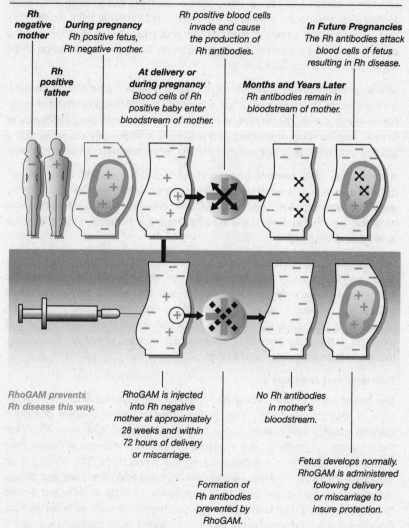

Rh negative mother

Rh positive father

During pregnancy
Rh positive fetus, Rh negative mother.

At delivery or during pregnancy
Blood cells of Rh positive baby enter bloodstream of mother.

Rh positive blood cells invade and cause the production of Rh antibodies.

Months and Years Later
Rh antibodies remain in bloodstream of mother.

In Future Pregnancies
The Rh antibodies attack blood cells of fetus resulting in Rh disease.

RhoGAM prevents Rh disease this way.

RhoGAM is injected into Rh negative mother at approximately 28 weeks and within 72 hours of delivery or miscarriage.

Formation of Rh antibodies prevented by RhoGAM.

No Rh antibodies in mother's bloodstream.

Fetus develops normally. RhoGAM is administered following delivery or miscarriage to insure protection.

RhoGAM® is a registered trademark of Johnson & Johnson

Identical twins come from the union of one egg and one sperm that for unknown reasons splits in two. These are called monozygotic twins. Monozygotic twins are always of the same sex. Fraternal twins come from two eggs fertilized by two different sperm and implanted in the uterus at the same time. These are known as dizygotic twins. Dizygotic twins can be of the same sex or one boy and one girl.

A mother carrying twins is often more uncomfortable than a mother carrying a single fetus. The presence of twins intensifies all of the conditions of pregnancy — indigestion, backache, varicose veins, sleeplessness, shortness of breath, and swelling of the feet and ankles. It is absolutely essential that a woman with a multiple pregnancy carefully follow her clinician's instructions.

It is not unusual for twins to be born about two to five weeks before the calculated due date. Extra clothing, diapers, cribs and bedding, as well as other essential baby supplies, should be prepared several weeks in advance. Extra help for the mother when she returns from the hospital should also be arranged beforehand.

Fetal reduction is most commonly used in women who have taken fertility drugs and are now carrying more than three viable fetuses. Because of the high risk of preterm delivery if all the fetuses are carried, some physicians reduce the number in order to improve the chances of delivering healthy babies. This procedure for multifetal reduction is performed later in the first trimester of the pregnancy at special centers where a physician, specifically trained in this procedure, is available.

Your age and pregnancy

The social trend in our society had been to marry young and have babies while a woman was in her 20s. Today however, many couples postpone starting a family until a woman is in her late 20s early 30s or even 40s. With the advances in medical care available today, most women, whatever their age, do not need to fear a difficult pregnancy and birth. Still, clinicians do recognize that women under 18 and over 35 need additional care and observation before, during and after their pregnancy, in order to reduce the risks to themselves and their babies. Though complications such as hypertension, diabetes and multiple births are more common in older pregnant women, a woman's health and level of fitness can affect her pregnancy more than her age. There may be additional tests performed, such as amniocentesis to more closely monitor the fetus. When planning your family, discuss your age with your doctor who is familiar with you and your medical history.

Down syndrome and the new ACOG guidelines

Down syndrome is caused by an error in cell division during the embryo's development that results in the production of an extra chromosome (number 21).

An infant born with this additional chromosome typically has developmental delays, a smaller head and in many cases, heart problems. The risk of a child being born with this condition gradually increases with the age of the mother.

Because of the potential risks associated with the invasive testing procedures of amniocentesis and chorionic villi sampling (CVS), age 35 was considered the threshold for offering these tests. Women under age 35 were encouraged to have a multiple marker screening (MMS) test during the second trimester to determine if they were at an increased risk to warrant these additional procedures.

In January of 2007, the American College of Obstetrics and Gynecology (ACOG) published new guidelines indicating that age 35 alone should no longer be used to determine which patients are screened versus those choosing amniocentesis or CVS. The guidelines also advise, "that all pregnant women, regardless of their age, should have the option of diagnostic testing. ACOG recognizes that a woman's decision to have an amniocentesis or CVS is based on many factors, such as a family or personal history of birth defects, the risk that the fetus will have a chromosome abnormality or an inherited condition, and the risk of pregnancy loss from an invasive procedure." [1]

These guidelines also mention improved first trimester testing procedures available at some centers. This includes a procedure known as nuchal translucency ultrasound measurement (page 55). This test measures the thickness of tissue behind the neck of the fetus. If the tissue is too thick, it may indicate an increased risk for Down syndrome.

The results may also be reviewed by your physician along with multiple marker tests performed during the second trimester. By reviewing tests from both the first and second trimester, your physician has a better opportunity for identifying a fetus "at risk" without creating the potential for too many expectant mothers to undergo an amniocentesis test.

[1] *ACOG News Release,* New Recommendations for Down Syndrome Call for Screening of All Pregnant Women, January 2, 2007. ACOG Office of Communications, 202-484-3321. communications@acog.org

Because the nuchal translucency ultrasound and first trimester blood test may not be available in all areas, it is important to understand and discuss your screening and diagnostic options for Down syndrome with your doctor.

Genetic disorders

One of the normal concerns of new parents is whether their child will be born with any flaws, or a tendency toward inherited diseases that may be passed to future generations. This concern is even greater if the couple already has a child with diabetes, Down syndrome, hemophilia, Tay-Sachs disease, a club foot, or cleft palate. The parents may be concerned about the possibility that such a genetic disorder may recur in any other children they conceive. For this reason it is important to obtain an accurate diagnosis of the problem and give your clinician detailed family histories of both the father and the mother (see page 180).

Without an accurate history, your doctor and other specialists cannot be as effective as possible. Don't allow fear or shame to conceal your worries about genetic problems. It is absolutely essential to obtain an accurate diagnosis of the condition, to evaluate all aspects of what having this condition means to a child, and to consider realistically the risk of having an affected child.

Additional prenatal tests are designed to detect certain genetic diseases or conditions. The need for additional tests may be determined by your age, medical or family history. Prenatal tests can include testing the chromosomes of the fetus.

Our chromosomes carry genetic information. Normally there are 46 chromosomes — 23 inherited from the mother and 23 from the father. The 23 from each parent are paired inside the nucleus of each human cell. Twenty-two of these pairs are not related to gender. The twenty-third pair of chromosomes are sex chromosomes. The XX chromosome is for a girl and the XY is a for boy. The child's gender is determined by the father. He can give either an X or a Y chromosone. A woman can only give an X. If the father gives the X chromosome the baby will be a girl. If he gives the Y chromosome the baby will be a boy.

Each person carries a few abnormal genes. Most often they do not cause a defect. The abnormal gene is cancelled out by the normal dominant gene.

Dominant disorders can be caused by a gene from either parent. The child of a parent having this altered gene has a 50 percent chance of inheriting the disorder. It is also possible that there can be a mutation (change) that causes a genetic disorder in the child's genes even if neither parent is a carrier.

Far more common are recessive disorders where one gene carrying the disorder is present in both the mother and father. When each parent is a carrier for the same recessive gene their children have one chance in four of having the disorder and one chance in two of being a carrier. If only one parent has the gene it is cancelled out by the normal dominant gene of the other parent. If you have the recessive gene for a certain disorder, you are a carrier for that disorder. Even though you show no sign of the disorder you can pass it on to your children. If only one of the parents has the recessive disorder and the other does not (and is not a carrier) your children have a 50 percent chance of being a carrier and no chance of having the disease.

Don't expect the clinician to know all the genetic answers immediately. He or she will frequently have to research the answer. In the case of a complex problem, the couple may be referred to a geneticist or a genetic laboratory for detailed investigation and evaluation.

Such an investigative workup may include ultrasound, amniocentesis, or chorionic villi sampling (CVS). (See pages 58-60.) These tests are capable of detecting in advance, some genetic problems or potential birth defects.

If you are at increased risk of having a genetic disorder, genetic counseling is recommended. Those at higher risk include:

• Couples who have already had a child with a birth defect.

• Couples with a history of genetic disorder in their family

• Women aged 35 or over.

Additionally, some racial and ethnic groups are associated with specific disorders. For example, Tay-Sachs disease is primarily associated with those of Jewish heritage; Sickle-Cell Anemia with African Americans; Beta-thalassemia, which causes anemia, is most common in persons of Mediterranean descent such as Italians and Greeks.

Some genetic disorders such as hemophilia are carried by the X-chromosome and called a sex-linked or X-linked disorder. This recessive disorder is carried by the mother but is rarely passed on to a daughter. If the father is normal there is a 50 percent chance that the son will be a hemophiliac. Individuals with hemophilia lack a substance needed for blood clotting. As a result, an injury or internal bleeding can be life threatening because the bleeding is difficult to stop.

Color blindness is a common X-linked trait. A woman may carry this gene on the X chromosome but the other X chromosome, which is dominant, cancels out the recessive one. But if this X chromosome is passed on to her son, and he does not have a dominant X chromosome he may be color blind.

Cystic fibrosis is another genetic disease most common among people of northern European descent. This disease affects primarily infants, children and young adults, causing severe respiratory symptoms. The American College of Obstetricians and Gynecologists (ACOG) now recommends that DNA screening for cystic fibrosis be made available to all couples seeking preconception or prenatal care, not just those with a personal or family history of carrying the cystic fibrosis gene.

A defect that is present at birth is called a congenital disorder whether the disorder is inherited or not. Genetic defects fall into three categories:

1. Chromosomal defect caused by a damaged, missing or extra chromosome.
2. Inherited defect caused by a gene that is passed from a parent to a child. This can be a result of a dominant, recessive or X-linked gene.
3. Multifactorial defect caused by a combination of factors.

Being a carrier does not mean you have the disease. It means that you carry the gene for it. Both parents would need to be carriers to place the baby at risk for having the disease. Most genetic counselors recommend that both parents undergo the blood tests for carrier status. Even if only one member of a couple is a carrier of a specific disease, the couple should both be tested.

Though certain genetic problems may be more common in one ethnic or racial group, the problem can still occur occasionally in another group.

Fetal Medicine

The relatively new field of fetal medicine has made progress in saving babies who at one time had little chance of survival. For example, the use of prenatal injections of corticosteroids to speed the development of the lungs and other organs of the fetus has reduced premature infant deaths by about

30 percent. In cases of severe anemia, a blood transfusion can be delivered directly into the fetus' blood stream. The most dramatic aspect of fetal medicine is fetal surgery. Though it poses greater risk to both the mother and the fetus it enables surgical correction of a number of congenital fetal defects such as spina bifida and urinary tract blockage.

Gestational Diabetes

Gestational diabetes develops during pregnancy and often disappears after the baby is born. This type of diabetes is one of the most frequent complications of pregnancy today.

When detected, usually in the middle of the pregnancy, it is essential that your blood sugar be brought to and maintained at normal levels so that your baby will not be affected. As a rule, gestational diabetes will recur with each following pregnancy.

You are at higher risk for gestational diabetes if you have a family history of diabetes or are overweight at the time of your pregnancy. Studies have shown that women who have had gestational diabetes are at increased risk for developing diabetes later in life. Having periodic checkups and keeping your weight within normal limits becomes essential.

High blood sugar can affect your fetus by crossing over the placenta. This is why it is so important, if you develop gestational diabetes, to follow your clinician's instructions carefully, for keeping your blood sugar within normal limits.

Risk factors include women:

- Over 25 years of age
- Who are overweight or obese
- Have a family history of diabetes
- Belong to an ethnic/racial group with a high incidence of diabetes (Hispanic, African American, Native American Asian)
- Previously delivered a baby weighing over 9 pounds or diagnosed with gestational diabetes in a previous pregnancy.

The American College of Obstetricians and Gynecologists and most healthcare professionals routinely order a glucose screening test on all of their pregnant patients when they are at 24 to 28 weeks gestation.

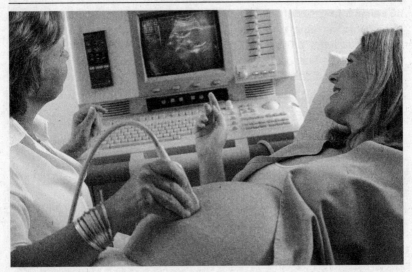

Office ultrasound procedure

Some women with gestational diabetes can control their blood sugar by diet alone. Others may need oral medication or insulin for the duration of the pregnancy. It is essential for both you and your baby to follow your clinician's advice closely. Do not limit your diet beyond what is recommended for you. Your baby needs sufficient calories and nutrition for normal development.

Many authorities use a two hour post-prandial (two hours after you eat) blood sugar of 120 mg/dl as the upper limit of "normal" blood glucose. Check with your healthcare provider regarding whether you should monitor your blood glucose levels yourself to see if your diet is properly controlling your glucose level, or if other medication is required.

Testing procedures

Ultrasound

Doctors can display a picture on a TV-like screen of the fetus in your uterus using sound waves which humans cannot hear. While you lie on a table, a technician passes a scanner over your abdomen aimed at your uterus. This ultrasonic scanner sends out sound waves which create different echoes as they encounter different types and densities of tissues. These echoes are shown on a TV screen as various patterns of light called a sonogram.

Although regular office ultrasound examinations may discover malformations (abnormalities) in the fetus, this is not the primary purpose for doing such an examination. Unless a patient is identified as a member of a high-risk group, referral to a specialist is normally not indicated.

Office ultrasound examination on obstetrical patients without high-risk indication, is performed primarily to evaluate gestational age, evaluate the growth and position of the fetus, and to verify the possibility of multiple births.

Ultrasound can also detect abnormalities such as a thickening behind the neck of the fetus called increased nuchal translucency. This can help determine if there is an added risk for genetic or chromosomal problems.

Ultrasound is usually performed between the 16th and 20th weeks. In special situations multiple ultrasound examinations may be indicated. Unlike X-Rays, there is no proven risk in ultrasound. It is noninvasive and causes no pain.

There are special situations where multiple ultrasound examinations may be indicated. The following conditions may require more than one ultrasound exam:

- If your clinician suspects the fetus is too large or too small for its gestational age
- If you are carrying twins or more
- If you are at increased risk for preterm labor (see page150)
- If you have any underlying medical condition such as diabetes or hypertension
- If your clinician suspects you have too much or too little amniotic fluid (see page 58)
- If you are bleeding

An ultrasound examination called a transvaginal ultrasound or sonogram uses a scanner or transducer probe inserted into the vagina. This helps your doctor view your pelvic organs and can also be used to measure the length of the cervical canal. It also is used to measure the size of your baby in the early months of pregnancy. An ultrasound examination with a vaginal probe is not painful.

A new form of ultrasound called Doppler velocimetry, views the uterus or baby to check the rate of blood flow.

Intrauterine growth restriction (IUGR)

IUGR can result in the birth of a baby who is considered small-for-gestational-age (SGA). In low-risk pregnancy, fetal growth is determined by measuring the fundal height — that is, from the top of the pubic bone to the top of the uterus. This measurement in centimeters approximately equals the number of weeks gestation. If your clinician finds this measurement is smaller than expected, an ultrasound exam may be recommended to more closely determine the fetus' growth.

During an ultrasound examination, measurements are taken of various fetal body parts to determine the approximate weight of the fetus. This weight is compared with the average weight for fetuses at the same gestational age. The average percentile is 50 although anything between the 10th and 90th percentile is considered within normal range. This means 10 percent of the population are smaller than normal (below the 10th percentile) and 10 percent are larger than normal (above the 90th percentile). This is not to say that all fetuses above and below the range are abnormal. What it does indicate to your clinician is that some may not be thriving and may need to be followed more closely.

The fetus whose estimated weight falls below the 10th percentile may have intrauterine growth restriction. The following are some of the possible causes of IUGR:

- There may be multiple fetuses.
- Some genetic factors may result in less than average fetal growth.
- Certain infections such as cytomegalovirus, measles or toxoplasmosis may have affected growth.
- Chromosomal abnormalities may have affected growth.
- Poor nutrition in the mother particularly in the third trimester.
- Smoking, alcohol, cocaine use or other environmental toxins have affected growth.

A fetus estimated to be above the 90th percentile may have macrosomia, that is, being large for gestational age (LGA). The possible causes of a LGA baby may be:

- The mother is a poorly controlled diabetic.
- The pregnancy has gone beyond 40 weeks gestation.

Amniocentesis

Amniocentesis is a test used to detect certain genetic disorders. The procedure is usually performed around the 16th to the 18th week of pregnancy and should not be any more painful than receiving an injection. It requires inserting a long, hollow needle through the mother's abdomen into the amniotic sac to obtain a sample of the amniotic fluid. The amniotic fluid contains cells generated by the fetus. These cells can be analyzed for chromosomal and chemical makeup to see if the twenty-three chromosome pairs are present and are normal in structure. This procedure can detect several abnormalities and growth patterns, among them Down syndrome and fetal lung maturity. Researchers are making progress today in detecting other potential disorders through analysis of the amniotic fluid.

The fluid sample also contains cells indicating the sex of the baby. This is important when a sex-linked hereditary disorder such as hemophilia is suspected. Amniocentesis is never performed simply to satisfy curiosity about a baby's sex.

When checking for genetic disorders, the cells from the amniotic fluid must be incubated. For this reason, test results can take up to three weeks. This waiting period can be the most difficult part of amniocentesis. It is reassuring to know that studies indicate approximately 95 percent of amniocentesis results are normal.

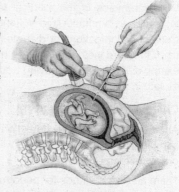

If you are Rh negative, you will be given an injection of Rhogam (see pages 46-47) following the amniocentesis to help prevent Rh sensitization.

Amniocentesis procedure

Amniocentesis is more accurate than ultrasound in detecting potential problems, but does have a higher risk. A study of over 28,000 amniocentesis procedures reported at a 2002 ACOG conference, found a fetal loss of 1 out of 327 procedures performed by obstetricians/gynecologists. Much of the risk has been reduced by using ultrasound to reveal the position of the fetus as the needle is inserted.

Amniotic fluid volume

The fetus grows within the amniotic sac, what is commonly called the "bag of water". This sac contains amniotic fluid. The volume of fluid increases until it reaches its maximum level at 34 weeks gestation. After that the fluid level gradually decreases in volume. Either a little more or a little less amniotic fluid is not usually a problem. However, large variations in amniotic fluid volume may be a symptom of a problem.

Oligohydramnios is the medical term for too little amniotic fluid. This can be the result of a rupture or tear in the membranes, allowing the fluid to leak out. This can indicate a problem with the mother and/or the fetus. If this happens and you are very close to your delivery date, your clinician may decide to deliver the baby. Or, the fetus may be monitored more closely, undergoing tests to assure its well being. You may be advised to stay off your feet and get more rest in order to improve blood flow to the uterus and placenta thus increasing the fetus' urine output resulting in an increase in amniotic fluid.

Polyhydramnios is the medical term for too much amniotic fluid. Larger increases in amniotic fluid volume may indicate a problem in the mother. Certain viral infections or diabetes in the mother can result in an increase in fluid. In rare cases, the increase may be due to a problem in the fetus. For example, if the fetus is having trouble swallowing fluid, more of it can accumulate in the sac.

Chorionic villi sampling (CVS)

Another test for the early detection of some genetic disorders is chorionic villi sampling or CVS. The chorionic villi are finger-like projections attached to the outermost fetal membrane.

There are two methods for performing a CVS procedure. One is the transcervical approach where a small catheter is inserted through the cervix while guided by ultrasound, to the villi where cells are collected from the developing

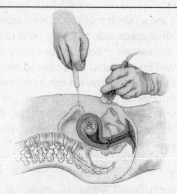

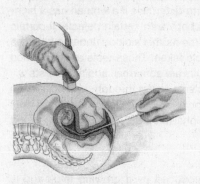

Transcervical CVS procedure   *Transabdominal CVS procedure*

placenta. The second technique is the transabdominal CVS. In this approach, after locally anesthetizing the skin, a needle is inserted through the abdominal wall, guided by ultrasound. This is a particularly useful alternative in women with vaginal infections such as genital herpes, gonorrhea or chlamydia. Transabdominal CVS is also indicated when the position of the placenta makes it difficult to reach through the cervix.

A woman who is Rh negative and undergoes CVS, should receive an injection of Rhogam following the procedure (see pages 45-47).

Although CVS reveals excellent information about many genetic disorders, it does not give any information about the development of the spinal cord.

CVS has two major advantages over amniocentesis. First, it can be performed at 10 to 12 weeks gestation as compared to amniocentesis which is performed at 16 to 18 weeks. And second, test results are available within one week while results from an amniocentesis may take 2 to 4 weeks. The anxiety of waiting to have an amniocentesis performed and the time it takes to get the results of this test can be very difficult for parents. An international randomized trial suggests that chorionic villi sampling may be safer and more efficient than early (11 weeks) amniocentesis. When the CVS procedure is compared with amniocentesis at 16 to18 weeks of pregnancy, it has a slightly higher rate of miscarriage. Discuss the advantages and risks with your clinician.

There are a number of blood tests used to determine if a woman has a higher-than-average risk of giving birth to a baby with certain defects. If certain birth defects are present, substances in the mother's blood undergo changes that can be detected in the blood sample taken. These tests are performed on all pregnant women. If initial test results are abnormal, additional tests will be performed. The most common problems found through maternal serum screening are neural tube defects, Down syndrome and abdominal wall defects. Maternal serum tests include alpha-fetoprotein (AFP) screening and multiple marker screening (MMS).

Alpha-fetoprotein (AFP) screening

A protein called alpha-fetoprotein is produced by a growing fetus and is present in fetal blood and in the amniotic fluid surrounding the fetus. A smaller amount of this protein crosses the placenta into the mother's blood. Abnormally high amounts found in the mother's blood sample during pregnancy can be an indication of a neural tube defect (NTD).

The brain and spinal cord of the embryo are formed in the first month of gestation. If problems arise during the time the brain and spinal cord are forming, an infant may be born without a brain or with spina bifida (split spine). A fetus with central nervous system problems will secrete large amounts of alpha-fetoprotein. This AFP can be detected in the mother's blood and in the amniotic fluid, although this test is not 100 percent foolproof.

Multiple marker screening

A common multiple marker screen (MMS) is called the "triple screen". It includes tests in addition to AFP which gives even more information about the risk of bearing a Down syndrome baby. This MMS test measures levels of the hormones human chorionic gonadotropin (hCG) and estriol in the mother's blood. A simple blood test can also provide this information. Levels of estriol are lower than normal when the fetus has Down syndrome. Levels of hCG, a hormone made by the placenta, are higher than normal when the fetus has Down syndrome.

Multiple marker screening is performed at 15 to 18 weeks gestation with the results available within 1 to 2 weeks. Unless the results of the three substances (AFP, hCG, and estriol) fall into the high-risk range, further testing will probably not be recommended by your clinician. These additional tests might include ultrasound and amniocentesis. Not all women whose multiple marker screening test show an increased risk for Down syndrome will have a baby with this defect. This test only predicts how likely a Down syndrome birth will be.

Researchers at the University of Alabama Medical College reported the addition of a test called inhibin A to the traditional triple marker maternal screening test in the second trimester. The quadruple screen calculates the risk of Down's syndrome from maternal age and the concentrations of maternal serum alpha-fetoprotein, unconjugated estriol, human chorionic gonadotropin and inhibin A. This test is performed between 14 and 22 weeks gestation and offers a more accurate means of detecting Down syndrome than the triple multiple marking screening test. This test can improve the detection rate for Down syndrome by 16 percent. However, the traditional triple marker screening test remains the most widely used test for Down syndrome.

Both the AFP and MMS tests are routinely offered to all pregnant women.

Non-stress and contraction stress tests

Two simple, inexpensive tests have been developed to help observe and monitor fetuses of post-date pregnancies that may be at risk.

The non-stress test is now the most widely used method of closely observing the fetus. In this test a monitor is placed over the woman's abdomen and the fetus's heartbeat is recorded. When the mother feels the fetus move or kick, she pushes a button to record the event. This test is based on the premise that the fetal heartbeat will increase with body movement, just as a healthy adult's heartbeat increases with exercise.

Sometimes the non-stress test is inconclusive or the clinician wants to see if the fetus can withstand the demands of labor. If this is the situation the contraction stress or oxytocin test may be performed. This test focuses on the fetal heartbeat as the fetus reacts to a uterine contraction, rather than to fetal movement. The mother is again hooked to a monitor, and the heartbeat is examined in relation to uterine contractions. Oxytocin is administered to stimulate contractions if there are no contractions, or, if they are not frequent enough. A pregnant women can also produce her own oxytocin by stimulating her nipples manually or with hot towels. Clinicians will occasionally use this method to stimulate uterine contractions.

Gestational stage	Test	Indication
10 to 12 weeks	Chorionic villi sampling (CVS)	To examine placental tissue for chromosomal and genetic diseases (see pages 58-59)
15 to 18 weeks	Amniocentesis	To test amniotic fluid for chromosomal and genetic diseases (see page 57)
16 to 18 weeks	Alfa-fetoprotein Screening (AFP) (see page 67)	To check blood to determine risk for neural tube disorders or Down syndrome (see page 60)
16 to 18 weeks	Multiple marker screening (MMS)	To measure hormone and AFP levels as a check to determine risk of Down syndrome (see page 60)
18 to 20 weeks	Ultrasound	To check the fetal growth, if a multiple pregnancy, some congenital abnormalities as well as a check for the position of the fetus and the placenta (see pages 54-56)
24 to 28 weeks	Glucose screening	To test for gestational diabetes (see page 54)
35 to 37 weeks	Group B streptococcus (GBS) screening	To test for GBS in mother who can pass it on to the baby during delivery (see pages 33-34)

Kick count

Your clinician may ask you to monitor the movements of your fetus. A common way of keeping track of fetal movements is to do what is called a "kick count." Ask your doctor what time of day you should do a kick count, then time how long it takes for the fetus to move 10 times (movement may feel like a kick, flutter, or a roll). Fetal movement varies, so it is not a good idea to compare the activity of your fetus with that of someone else. If you have been advised to do a kick count, your doctor or other health professional will give you specific instructions, including how often it should be done and at what point you should call your clinician.

The purpose of doing kick counts is to help identify a potential problem at its earliest stage.

Biophysical profile

The biophysical profile is a combination of the non-stress test with ultrasound to examine muscle tone, fetal movement, fetal breathing and the amount of amniotic fluid surrounding the fetus. Though the fetus gets oxygen through the placenta, there are chest wall movements (fetal breathing) monitored in the profile.

Each of the preceding factors is given a numerical rating or score and this score is totaled. A score of 8 to 10 is normal. If the score is below this range, further testing may be required. This non-stress/ultrasound test takes about 30 minutes. It is not harmful to the fetus and can be repeated as needed. The results of the biophysical profile will help your clinician determine whether you need special care or an early delivery.

Percutaneous umbilical cord blood sampling (PUBS)

This test is performed by using a very fine long needle, directed continuously by ultrasound, to obtain a blood sample from the umbilical cord close to where it is attached to the placenta. In this test, doctors can check for some genetic diseases or anemia using a sample of the blood from the fetus. This test does have risks, and is not available in every area.

Summary

These tests are by no means the only screening procedures available. Your doctor may recommend other tests, in addition to, or instead of, the ones discussed here. It must be emphasized that not all of these tests are routine or performed automatically. They are a means of evaluating possible problems and assessing fetal growth and development when problems are suspected. Pregnancy is a normal, healthy part of life for a woman. Yet, at the same time it is complex enough to justify careful monitoring for the sake of both the mother and the baby. If your clinician recommends any of the screening processes outlined in this book, or any other testing procedures, ask about the benefits and risks. You must take the responsibility to know and understand the reasons for the procedures.

Modern medicine has reduced many of the dangers and discomforts of pregnancy. These tests are one of the ways this has been accomplished.

Chapter 6 Your weight and your diet

OUR SOCIETY PUTS A GOOD DEAL OF EMPHASIS on weight control, and most expectant mothers are concerned about how much weight they will gain during pregnancy. So, how much weight should you gain during pregnancy?

The answer to the question can be more clearly understood by first looking at the weight required to create a new baby.

Weight Distribution (in pounds)	
The average baby weighs	7½
The placenta	1½
Increased fluid volume	4
Increased weight of uterus	2
Increased weight of breast tissue	2
Increased blood volume	4
Maternal stores of nutrients	7
Amniotic fluids	2
Total	30

Naturally, as an individual, you may deviate from this average. A weight gain of about 25 to 35 pounds is recommended by the American College of Obstetricians and Gynecologists for a woman of normal weight at the beginning of her pregnancy. Women who are underweight should gain near the top of the range, while women who are markedly overweight should gain less, about 15 to 20 pounds Whatever your weight gain, it is important to eat a nutritious diet to ensure adequate nutrients for you and your fetus.

As we all know, it is easy for most people to gain weight. When you are pregnant you need to focus on gaining only what you need. Unnecessary weight contributes to several physical difficulties. Your legs and back, unaccustomed to the heavy load, may develop aches and pains. A rapid, excessive weight gain can increase your blood pressure and put an extra strain on your heart. The extra weight may make moving about more difficult, increasing the possibility that you could trip and fall. Finally, your extra weight can make labor and delivery more difficult. It's a fallacy that gaining extra weight means you will have a larger baby. It simply means there will be a larger mother after your baby is born!

Controlling your diet

Throughout your pregnancy, you and your baby will need sufficient nourishment to stay healthy. This means that you must maintain a well-rounded diet with a regulated consumption of calories. More than ever before, you will need to control your diet and to exercise discipline over the quality of the foods that you eat.

Unfortunately, too many mothers-to-be have developed poor eating habits. Often these begin during their years in high school and continue into their adult lives. Studies of pregnant women indicate that these "starvation" diets can have serious consequences for the next generation. The fast food craze consisting of hamburgers, french fries, pizza, and soft drinks does not provide adequate nourishment for the pregnant woman and her fetus. If you have fallen into the habit of relying on such a diet, it is essential for you to develop new and healthier eating habits during your pregnancy. Here are three good reasons for you to maintain a healthy diet:

1. Your body will be building new tissues in the fetus, and your body will also be losing some cells to the new life that is growing within you. You need adequate nourishment for both building new tissues and replenishing those lost cells.

2. Both you and your fetus need a supply of vitamins and minerals.

3. Certain foods are necessary to keep your kidneys and intestines functioning properly and for maintaining overall good health. Both kidneys and intestines are overworked during pregnancy.

When we talk about controlling your diet, what do we mean? We mean eating a balanced daily diet of foods from each of the basic food groups. We also mean consuming enough calories for you and your fetus but not an abundant quantity of calories.

The American College of Obstetricians and Gynecologists (ACOG) suggests the following food guidelines:

	Number of servings		Number of servings
Milk	4	**Fruits and vegetables** (total)	5
		Vitamin C	2
Protein (total)	3-4	Vitamin A	2
Animal	2-3	Other	1
Legumes/nuts	1-2	**Whole grain products**	4
		Others	

Food Pyramid

For many years the U.S. Department of Agriculture (USDA) used the pyramid structure shown below to indicate the daily dietary recommendations for each of the main food groups. Though it provides some good basic information, the USDA recognized there were some limitations in the presentation. As a result, in April 2005 they introduced MyPyramid, an "interactive food guidance system."

MyPyramid.gov
STEPS TO A HEALTHIER YOU

By visiting the Web site, mypyramid.gov, individuals can learn more about the new government guidelines. The interactive feature of the site enables you to enter information for your age, gender, weight and level of physical activity to develop your own dietary plan. The goal of the interactive MyPyramid is to encourage personalization, physical activity, variety and proportionality more effectively than the earlier guidelines.

Source: U.S. Department of Agriculture

Use sparingly
fats, oils and sweets

2-3 servings
from dairy products

2-3 servings
from meat, poultry,
fish, dry beans, eggs,
and nut group

6-11 servings
of complex carbohydrates
which include bread,
cereal, rice and
pasta group

2-4 servings
from the
fruit groups

3-5 servings
from vegetable
group

Calorie intake

A calorie is a measurement that expresses how much energy food produces. An average non-pregnant woman burns approximately 2000 calories each day. If your diet provides approximately 2000 calories each day then you'll maintain a constant weight. But if you eat more, or richer foods with 3500 calories a day then you have an excess 1500 calories that aren't burned off and become fat. If you consume fewer calories than you need every day you'll lose weight. Knowing the number of calories your body requires and consuming that amount is the only sensible way to control weight.

At the beginning of your pregnancy, assuming you are the proper weight for your age and height, you should keep you caloric intake at approximately 2300 calories per day. Toward the end of pregnancy the demands of your baby will increase the energy your body needs from the food it burns. At that time your caloric intake may rise to as high as 2600 calories a day. However, late in pregnancy, you may not be as active as you were in which case your caloric intake may not need to be increased.

What foods should you eat?

These simple guidelines will help you in planning meals to take advantage of the wide variety of foods that supply essential proteins, vitamins, minerals, carbohydrates, and calcium.

Meat – Eight ounces daily of lean meat, preferably chicken or turkey. Many clinicians recommend red meat only twice a week because of its higher cholesterol content.

Fish – Fish are an excellent source of protein. They are generally high in B vitamins and low in saturated fat, but high in Omega-3 fatty acids, believed to reduce the risk of heart disease. When prepared baked or broiled, rather than fried, fish are lower in calories. However, there are some precautions to take when selecting fish.

In an October 1988 issue of the Nutrition Action Healthletter, a recommendation was made that pregnant women, and women who are breastfeeding limit the fish they eat to ocean fish caught offshore because of the amount of ocean pollution near the shoreline and among inland lakes (even the

Great Lakes). Because exposure to mercury is particularly damaging to the fetus and nursing infant, it is advisable to limit the amount of tuna you eat to one-half pound per week. For specific recommendations on which fish to avoid, contact your local, state or county health department. The Food and Drug Administration (FDA) now recommends that women of childbearing age, nursing moms and children under the age of five avoid eating fish known to contain high levels of methyl mercury, including shark, swordfish, king mackerel and tilefish. Smaller fish such as bass, salmon and shellfish are considered safe to eat.

Milk – Four 8-ounce cups of milk each day. Portions of this may be consumed as cocoa, milk base soups, custards and with cereal.

Cheese – One ounce daily of American, Swiss or other solid cheese. Cream cheese and cheese spreads do not have the same food value in small quantities as do the bulk cheeses.

Eggs – It's widely recognized that cracked eggs could be contaminated with Salmonella, an organism that is known to cause food poisoning. An article in the October 1988 publication of Nutrition Action Healthletter reported researchers' suspicion that Salmonella can be found in un-cracked eggs as well. It is believed that the organism has contaminated the hen's ovaries which contained the yolks before the shells of the eggs were formed.

Salmonella is destroyed by thorough cooking. The Centers for Disease Control (CDC) in Atlanta, Georgia recommends the following:

- Avoid foods made with raw or undercooked eggs such as Caesar salad, hollandaise sauce, eggnog or homemade ice cream. Some restaurants have eliminated the coddled egg (1 minute egg) from their Caesar salad dressing. Ask the server or chef before ordering.

- Boil eggs for 7 minutes, poach for 5 minutes or fry for 3 minutes on each side.

- Do not eat eggs "sunny side up" (not turned). Tests have shown the Salmonella bacteria survive even if the eggs are overcooked on only one side. Because of the cholesterol content, some clinicians recommend no more than four or five eggs per week. Eggs may be counted with other foods such as French toast.

Recommended Daily Dietary Allowances for Adolescent and Adult, Pregnant and Lactating Women

	14-18 yrs	Pregnant 19-30 yrs	31-50 yrs	14-18 yrs	Lactating 19-30 yrs	31-50 yrs
Fat-soluble vitamins						
Vitamin A	750 µg	770 µg	770 µg	1200 µg	1300 µg	1300 µg
Vitamin D	5 µg	5 µg	5 µg	5 µg	5 µg	5 µg
Vitamin E	15 mg	15 mg	15 mg	19 mg	19 mg	19 mg
Vitamin K	75 µg	90 µg	90 µg	75 µg	90 µg	90 µg
Water-soluble vitamins						
Vitamin C	80 mg	85 mg	85 mg	115 mg	120 mg	120 mg
Thiamin	1.4 mg	1.4 mg	1.4 mg	1.4 mg	1.4 mg	1.4 mg
Riboflavin	1.4 mg	1.4 mg	1.4 mg	1.6 mg	1.6 mg	1.6 mg
Niacin	18 mg	18 mg	18 mg	17 mg	17 mg	17 mg
Vitamin B_6	1.9 mg	1.9 mg	1.9 mg	2 mg	2 mg	2 mg
Folate (folic acid)	600 µg	600 µg	600 µg	500 µg	500 µg	500 µg
Vitamin B_{12}	2.6 µg	2.6 µg	2.6 µg	2.8 µg	2.8 µg	2.8 µg
Minerals						
Calcium	1300 mg	1000 mg	1000 mg	1300 mg	1000 mg	1000 mg
Phosphorus	1240 mg	700 mg	700 mg	1250 mg	700 mg	700 mg
Iron	27 mg	27 mg	27 mg	10 mg	9 mg	9 mg
Zinc	13 mg	11 mg	11 mg	14 mg	12 mg	12 mg
Iodine	220 µg	220 µg	220 µg	290 µg	290 µg	290 µg
Selenium	60 µg	60 µg	60 µg	70 µg	70 µg	70 µg

Recommendations measured as Adequate Intake (AI) instead of Recommended Daily Dietary Allowance (RDA). An AI is set instead of an RDA if insufficient evidence is available to determine an RDA. The AI is based on observed or experimentally determined estimates of average nutrient intake by a group (or groups) of healthy people.

Data from Institute of Medicine. Dietary reference intakes for calcium, phosphorus, magnesium, vitamin D, and fluoride. Washington, DC: National Academy Press; 1997. Institute of Medicine (US). Dietary reference intakes from thiamin, riboflavin, niacin, vitamin B_6, folate, vitamin B_{12}, pantothenic acid, biotin, and choline. Washington, DC: National Academy Press; 1998. Institute of Medicine (US). Dietary reference intakes for vitamin C, vitamin E, selenium, and carotenoids. Washington, DC: National Academy Press; 2000. Institute of Medicine (US). Dietary reference intakes for vitamin A, vitamin K, arsenic, boron, chromium, copper, iodine, iron, manganese, molybdenum, nickel, silicon, vanadium, and zinc. Washington, DC: National Academy Press; 2002.

These are some essential energy and nutrient foods:

Salads – You should eat two cupfuls of fresh green leafy raw vegetables and other colored vegetables each day. These include lettuce, carrots, cucumbers, celery, tomatoes, and other cold salad ingredients.

Vegetables – Besides raw vegetables, cooked vegetables should be included once a day. An 8-ounce serving of asparagus, beans, broccoli, peas, spinach, carrots, brussels sprouts, or turnips will supply essential iron and vitamins to your diet. Cooking should be brief. Preferably steamed or using only a small amount of boiling water, so the nutritious elements will be retained. Fresh produce, properly cooked is best, but frozen and canned vegetables may be used.

Cereal – Any of the whole wheat, rice and grain cereals whether hot or cold, should be served once a day. One slice of whole wheat bread may be substituted for one serving of cereal.

Bread – Whole wheat bread is more nutritious than ordinary white bread. Two or three slices daily will supply ample nutrients without adding unnecessary calories. Fortified pastas can be substituted in moderation.

Fats – Fat is an integral part of all body tissues. It provides energy for body functions and is required as a vehicle for getting the fat-soluble vitamins (A, D, E and K) to the tissues. Although its role is important, no minimum requirements have been established. Many foods, including meats, nuts, eggs, and some dairy products contain significant amounts of fat. Additional fat in the form of oil, margarine, or butter are often added during the preparation and serving of foods. It has been suggested that no more than 30 percent of the calories in your diet come from fat, and that at least two-thirds of those come from unsaturated, polyunsaturated and monounsaturated sources. Examples of these are Soybean, cottonseed, safflower and olive oils.

Fruit – Oranges, grapefruits, lemons, tomatoes, tangerine, melons, pineapples and strawberries should be served once or twice a day. Juices of any of these fruits are also good.

Limit these foods:

Starches – If extra calories are a problem for you, decrease the serving size of potatoes, noodles, rice, corn, lima beans, spaghetti and macaroni, perhaps adding them to your diet only a few times per week. These foods are nutritious, but are fairly high in calories despite the amount of essential energy they can provide.

Desserts – Rich cakes, pastries, candy and to a lesser extent, ice cream and nuts, are essentially empty calorie sources and should be avoided, or at least kept to a minimum. Lower calorie, desserts such as ice milk, custard, and milk puddings can be more nutritious and satisfy a desire for sweets.

Liquids

You need 2 quarts (8 glasses) of liquid a day. This can include water, milk and juices. Alcohol should be eliminated entirely during your pregnancy. It's best not to count coffee and tea as part of your liquids since you should be limiting your consumption of these during pregnancy.

What not to eat

Common sense should tell you to avoid foods that normally cause you digestive difficulties. In most instances, a substitute can be found for any recommended food you may dislike. Don't be surprised if some of your favorite foods will have to be avoided for a while. Rich foods may create heartburn and stomach upset. Other possible offenders include fried foods, sausage, and fish with high oil content such as smoked fish, herring, tuna and salmon. You should avoid foods such as sushi (raw fish) as well as raw or very rare meat. These uncooked or undercooked protein sources may contain bacteria or parasites. Proper cooking destroys these. Cook your food medium-well to well done.

Although some women may be advised to reduce their use of salt, most pregnant women do not need to change their seasoning habits provided they are in good health and their pregnancy is progressing normally. Sodium is a necessary ingredient in a pregnant woman's diet. While moderation, particularly in the use of salt and the consumption of excessively salted foods is appropriate for everyone, severe restriction of salt is not advisable since both you and your fetus have increased needs for sodium at this time.

Food Additives

Check with your doctor before using any sugar substitutes. Cyclamates have been banned in the United States and Canada. The sweetener aspartame, commercially known as Equal or Nutrasweet, is composed of two amino acids, phenylalanine and aspartic acid, that appear naturally in many foods. Although most people can eat these amino acids without any problems, high levels of phenylalanine in the blood of women with phenylketonuria (PKU) may harm the nervous systems of these women and/or their unborn babies. PKU is an inborn condition in which the body is unable to use phenylalanine properly, thus allowing accumulation of the amino acid in body fluid. The results may be mental retardation and other nervous system disorders.

All of this can be prevented by a diet low in phenylalanine. Thus, women with PKU should not use the sweetener aspartame. As a general precaution, all pregnant women should consider limiting or eliminating this sweetener until more is known about the effects of it on a pregnant woman and her fetus. As a precaution, government warning labels have been added to artificially sweetened products limiting their use to diabetics and others who must curtail their use of sugars. During pregnancy and breastfeeding the use of artificial sweeteners for the purpose of calorie reduction is a questionable practice. Pregnant women obviously should avoid any unnecessary exposure to materials that might harm the fetus.

The sweetener sucralose has been approved by the Food and Drug Administration (FDA). It is about 600 times sweeter than sugar. So far the FDA has not found any evidence that it has any toxic side effects. Sucralose does not break down when heated. According to the manufacturer, Johnson & Johnson, no warning labels are required and no segment of the population is excluded from using this sugar substitute.

Nitosamines

Nitrosamines are potent carcinogens (cancer causing agents) in animals. Since humans are often affected in similar ways, there is concern about nitrosamines in our food supply. While they are rarely found in food, certain food additives can be readily converted into nitrosamines when combined with other chemicals. Two of the most common are sodium nitrite and sodium nitrate, which are added to cured and smoked meats and fish. Nitrate, which may be broken down to nitrite, is sometimes found in leafy green vegetables, particularly when nitrate fertilizers are used. The wise approach is to avoid highly processed foods and to thoroughly wash all fruits and vegetables.

It is difficult to be aware of every potential problem, but sticking to a varied diet of quality foods may be the most sensible course of action.

Why certain foods are important

It is important to understand why special nutritional needs must be met during pregnancy. You'll be expending more energy for both you and the fetus. This will require more calories. But these should be calories that supply the additional nutrients you need, not simply empty calories.

Proteins – The protein you eat is broken down by your body into amino acids, sometimes called the "building blocks of life." There are some 20 amino acids known to exist in food, but only eight of these are considered essential amino acids. This means that these essential amino acids must be supplied from dietary sources since the body itself is not equipped to produce them. The remaining 12 amino acids, however, can be manufactured by your body.

During pregnancy your need for protein increases significantly. Protein plays an integral role in the growth and maintenance of your own tissues to support pregnancy as well as the growth of the fetus. Studies suggest that an increase in protein of about 10 grams a day is desirable in pregnancy. That means that the recommended daily allowance (RDA) for most pregnant women would be about 60 grams a day. Many nutritionists and clinicians, however, feel that protein intake should be higher — even up to 90 grams a day — especially in the last part of the pregnancy.

Protein is available from a variety of ordinary foods, especially animal sources such as red meats, poultry, fish, eggs, and dairy products. These sources are often called "complete" proteins. That is, they contain all of the 8 essential amino acids. Protein is also found in vegetable or plant sources, but this protein usually lacks one or more of the eight essential amino acids. That is why these sources are called "incomplete" proteins. To overcome this and achieve the necessary amounts of protein you can combine foods to form a complete protein source (see pages 88-89; 90 for information about vegetarian diets).

Carbohydrates – Like fat, no minimum level of carbohydrate intake has been set. Although it is suggested that carbohydrates make up 55 percent or more of your daily diet, with simple sugars just a small portion. Carbohydrate is widely distributed in foods, particularly those of vegetable origin, therefore, a carbohydrate-free diet would be truly difficult to achieve. If you were successful, the diet would almost certainly lead to malnutrition and shortages of several vitamins, especially B complex and C. Very low carbohydrate diets have been associated with abnormal metabolism and eventually several kinds of diseases. Many people feel, however, that the average person would

Food Groups

Milk group: for calcium, protein, Vitamin A and D, riboflavin

- 1 cup fluid whole, 1%, 2%, skim milk or equivalents
- 1 cup yogurt
- ½ cup evaporated milk
- 4 tbsp non-fat dry milk
- 1 cup custard or other milk based dessert

- 1 cup cream soup, made with milk
- 1 ¾ cup ice cream
- 1½ cup cottage cheese
- 1½ oz. cheddar cheese[1]
- 1 cup soybean milk[2]
- ¾ cup tofu[2] (soybean curd)

Meat Group: for protein, iron and Vitamin B

Animal protein:
- 3 oz lean meat (veal, beef, lamb, pork), fish or seafood, poultry, or variety meats (kidney, heart, liver)
- 2 eggs
- 3 oz cheddar cheese
- ¾ cup cottage cheese
- ½ cup tuna

Legumes and nuts:
- ¾ cup dried beans or peas (cooked)
- 4 tbsp peanut butter
- 1 oz nuts or sunflower seeds
- ¾ cup tofu
- ¾ cup garbanzo, lima, kidney beans, lentils

Whole grain products: [4] for carbohydrates, B vitamins, iron and some protein

- 1 slice bread
- 1 roll, dumpling, muffin, or biscuit
- 5 saltine crackers
- 2 graham crackers
- ¾ cup ready-to-eat cereal
- ¾ cup cooked cereal

- ¾ cup cooked corn meal, grits, rice, macaroni, noodles, or spaghetti
- 2 corn tortillas
- 1 large flour tortilla
- 1 tbsp wheat germ

[1] Count cheese as a meat or milk, not both simultaneously.
[2] Lacks vitamin B_{12}; if used often, be sure to include other sources of this nutrient
[3] Vegetable oils such as sunflower, cottonseed and margarines made from them are good sources of vitamin E.

benefit from decreasing his or her intake of sucrose or other refined sugars. These include white or brown sugar, molasses, honey and even so-called "raw" sugars. In place of these refined sugars should be a greater intake of complex carbohydrates (starches) as found in cereals, pasta, grains, breads, vegetables, and fruits. This dietary change is known to result in decreased sucrose intake and consequently, reduced incidence of tooth decay It also provides increased fiber or roughage in the diet that promotes improved

Fruit and vegetable group: for minerals, vitamins and roughage

Vitamin C
- ¾ cup orange or other citrus juice or enriched fruit drink
- ½ large grapefruit
- ½ cantaloupe, guava, mango, or papaya
- 1 large orange
- 1 cup strawberries

- 1½ cup pineapple juice
- ¾ cup chopped green (or chili) peppers
- 2 tomatoes
- 1½ cup tomato juice
- ¾ cup cooked broccoli, brussel sprouts, raw cabbage, bok choy, cooked collards, kale, mustard, greens, spinach, turnip greens

Vitamin A
- ¾ cup asparagus, bok choy, broccoli, brussel sprouts, chard, collards, cress, kale, spinach, turnip greens, or other dark green leaves, cooked
- 1 cup of any of the above, raw

- ¾ cup cooked pumpkin, carrots, winter squash, sweet potato, or yam
- 1 cup carrots
- 4 fresh apricots
- ½ large cantaloupe

Other fruits and vegetables
- ¾ cup potato or other not listed above
- 3 plums
- 6 prunes
- 8 dates
- ¾ cup other fruit

- 1 large apple
- 1½ bananas
- 1 large peach or pear
- ¾ cup berries, grapes, or raisins

Others: for additional calories
- 1 cup non-milk and non-juice beverages
- Sweets (pastry, cookies, cakes, pies)

- 1 tbsp fats (margarine, butter, mayonnaise, vegetable oil [3])
- Condiments (catsup, mustard, sauces)

[4] *Whole grain products are richer source of vitamin E, vitamin B[6], folacin acid, phosphorous, magnesium, and zinc than enriched/refined products. At least 75 percent of your daily servings should be met from whole grain sources to help meet your need for these nutrients.*

bowel function. There may be other benefits as well. Recent research indicates that fiber may play a significant role in controlling the rate at which foods are digested and absorbed from the intestine. At the present time there are no known risks to this type of dietary modification.

Fats – Just as an excess of fat in the diet is unwise, a fat-free diet would not be conducive to good health either. Fat provides energy for body functions and is necessary to convey the fat-soluble vitamins (A, D, E, and K) to the body's tissues. Although its role is important, no minimum requirements have been established. Nevertheless, the typical diet often contains too much fat. Many are concerned as well about fat from animal sources, called saturated fat, that may play a role in some disease processes. It has been suggested that no more than 30 percent of the calories in your diet come from fat and that at least half of these are derived from unsaturated, polyunsaturated or monounsaturated sources. Examples of these are soybean, cottonseed, sunflower and olive oils. Fat is also a concentrated source of calories, and if weight control is a problem, cutting back on fats is recommended.

Since you do not want to consume excess fats yet you cannot entirely eliminate fats from your diet, try to strike a happy medium. Avoid foods that are high in fat but contain little or no amounts of other nutrients. Typically sauces and pastries that are often high in refined sugar but contain few vitamins and minerals. On the other hand, there are many foods such as cheese and eggs that are high in fat yet can make a significant contribution to your nutrition.

Although the fat substitute Olestra has been approved by the FDA for use in snacks there is evidence that Olestra, as it passes through the gastrointestinal tract, robs the body of the fat-soluble vitamins A, D, E, K, and beta carotene. It is also known to produce side effects such as diarrhea and cramping. It is best to avoid foods containing Olestra.

Vitamins

Vitamins such as A, B, B_1, B_2, C, D, E and K are essential to maintain the cells and tissues of mother and fetus. They exist in varying proportions in most of the foods listed in your daily intake. To assure that you receive ample supplies, vitamins may be prescribed as a supplement by your clinician. Remember, however, that vitamin supplements should not be substituted for food. In fact, vitamin supplements are ineffective unless taken with food.

Also, the fact that vitamin and mineral supplements safeguard your health and your baby's well-being does not mean that taking more than is prescribed is better. Some vitamins can be dangerous in large doses. For example, Vitamins A and D can be toxic if taken in large quantities. Therefore, take only the dose of vitamin and mineral supplements that your clinician recommends.

Though vitamin A is important in maintaining an adequate diet and is essential to normal reproduction, recent studies have found that too much vitamin A may cause birth defects. Women of childbearing age should be aware of the danger of excessive amounts of vitamin A.

It is far better for women of childbearing age to get their vitamin A from beta-carotene found in fruits and vegetables. Beta-carotene found in plant food has not been shown to cause vitamin A toxicity. The dietary allowance of vitamin A is not increased during pregnancy (see table on page 69).

Calcium and iron

Healthy bone tissue requires calcium, much of it supplied by milk and related dairy products. When your fetus' bones are growing and strengthening during the last months of pregnancy, your clinician may recommend augmenting your diet with calcium supplements in the form of tablets, chewable tablets, or a liquid. There is evidence that women with a history of high blood pressure before their pregnancies as well as women with poor nutritional status, should receive calcium carbonate supplements before and during pregnancy. Avoid calcium supplements based on bone meal, dolomite or oyster shell because of the risk of lead contamination.

An iron supplement may also be recommended. The reason is that it may be difficult for a pregnant woman to meet the requirement for iron by diet alone. The recommended intake (RI) for pregnant women is 25 mg per day. This iron is needed for the mother's increased blood volume, placenta, and the needs of the fetus. One way to increase the amount of iron absorbed from iron-containing foods is to eat a food rich in vitamin C at the same meal. For example, a generous serving of broccoli served with a pork chop will allow your body to make better use of the iron content of the meat. You can also raise the iron content in foods by cooking in iron pots and skillets.

Other minerals

Minerals are needed by your body as a part of structural compounds, for example, calcium in bone or as helpers in a variety of chemical reactions. In addition to calcium and iron other important minerals include sodium, potassium, iodine, phosphorus, and zinc. Some minerals, sodium, potassium, and phosphorus, are readily available through common food sources. Others are more difficult to obtain in the necessary amounts (iron, calcium and zinc.) As a general rule, if you make reasonably sound food choices and eat a variety of foods, you will probably meet most mineral requirements before, during, and after pregnancy. The one exception is iron, which as explained earlier is needed in greater amounts during pregnancy and which is found in relatively limited amounts in the typical diet.

Vegetarian diet

For various reasons, many people prefer to omit meat, poultry, and fish from their diets and become vegetarians. Such a diet can be continued through pregnancy, but the vegetarian who is pregnant must be absolutely certain that all her nutritional needs are met. Careful planning is the key to insuring adequate nutrition for those adhering to a vegetarian diet. A major concern is the quantity and quality of protein, but the total dietary intake, including vitamins and minerals, must also be considered. Vegetarians can be well nourished if a variety of plant foods are eaten. Be sure to include foods rich in calcium, vitamin A, and riboflavin as well as sources of vitamin B_2 and vitamin D. Milk and eggs are espe-
cially recommended for pregnant and breastfeeding women. They help meet requirements for vitamins A and D (if fortified milk is used), vitamin B_2, calcium, and riboflavin, all of which are needed in greater quantities by both the growing fetus and the mother.

There are a few guidelines for developing a nutritious diet if meat, poultry, and fish are omitted.

- Compliment incomplete plant proteins with each other and with dairy foods. Plant protein is often deficient in one or more amino acids, the building blocks of protein. Thus, plant proteins may be called "incomplete." Fortunately, various types of plant proteins are deficient in different amino acids, so that they may be combined to complement each other. That is, the deficiencies of one food are complemented by the strengths of another (see table on page 80).

- Increase your intake of legumes, dried seeds, and nuts for protein and iron.

- Increase your intake of dairy foods for calcium, protein, and vitamin B12. Insufficient vitamin B_{12}, an inherent problem in strict vegetarian diets during pregnancy and breastfeeding, has been reported to result in some cases, in failure to thrive and developmental delay in infants and young children.

- Eliminate or reduce by at least half, "empty" calories in sugars, concentrated sweets, and visible fats.

- Increase intake of whole grain breads and cereals for B vitamins, protein, and iron.

- Increase intake of fruits and vegetables for vitamins A and C and for minerals.

If you are on a vegetarian diet or any other special diet, discuss your nutritional needs and how you can meet them with your clinician.

About food cravings

It is true that pregnant women do sometimes have desires for unusual foods such as pickles, ice cream, strawberries, or melons out of season. Researchers have found, however, that everyone has food cravings once in a while, not just pregnant women. The cravings of pregnant women are probably intensified because of special emotional or physical circumstances. A pregnant woman may ask for a special food or for greater amounts of a favorite food if she is excited, fearful, or upset about some aspect of her pregnancy. Occasionally, a craving may indicate a nutritional need. For example, a desire for an orange may suggest her body needs vitamin C.

Complementary protein sources

Protein Pair	Example
Legumes	Black beans and rice Kidney bean tacos Soybean curd, rice, and greens
Legumes plus seeds	Split pea soup with sesame crackers Garbanzo and sesame seed spread Peanut and sunflower seed tacos
Legumes plus nuts	Dry roasted soybeans and almonds Chili garbanzos and mixed nuts
Grains plus milk	Oatmeal and milk Macaroni and cheese Bulgur wheat and yogurt
Legumes plus seeds plus milk	Garbanzo beans and sesame seeds in cheese sauce
Legumes plus nuts plus milk	Mixed beans and slivered almonds with yogurt dressing
Legumes plus milk	Lentil soup made with milk, peanuts and cheese cubes
Seeds or nuts plus milk*	Sesame seeds mixed with cottage cheese Chopped walnuts rolled in semi-hard cheese
Legumes plus egg	Cooked black eye peas with egg salad
Grains plus egg	Buckwheat (kasha) made with egg
Grains plus egg plus milk	Potato kugel Rice and raisin custard cheese muffin
Seeds plus egg plus milk	Cheese omelette with sesame seeds

*Protein quality may not be as good as the other milk "pairs."

Pica

The compulsive eating of a non-food substance such as dirt, clay or corn-starch is called Pica. Pica and unusual food cravings seem to be more common in pregnant women. Pica may also occur in patients with an iron or zinc deficiency and is found more frequently among certain cultural groups.

Eating Disorders

Two major eating disorders are anorexia nervosa and bulimia. Anorexia is characterized by a loss or lack of appetite with a refusal to maintain a normal minimal body weight, and with an intense fear of becoming fat, even feeling fat when extremely emaciated (thin). Bulimia is characterized by binge eating followed by self-induced vomiting.

New studies have found that the effects of the mother's eating disorder on the fetus can be devastating. Anorexia has been shown to result in multiple complications in both the mother and the fetus. In bulimic patients, the risk of fetal loss is twice that of normal pregnant women.

Chapter 7 Maintaining a healthy lifestyle

*T*O COMPETE SUCCESSFULLY IN ANY SPORT, an athlete must prepare his or her body to accomplish the goal. In many ways you are similar to an athlete. Like the athlete, you must go through a training period in which you exercise, get sufficient rest, and modify your normal lifestyle.

Instead of an athletic competition, you will be preparing to create a new human being. The success of your training period should make your delivery easier and your baby healthier. You'll be giving your child a solid start in life, and you will look and feel better yourself. Let's look at the guidelines you need to follow during this period and see how they can make you and your baby both winners.

Resting

During the first few months of your pregnancy you may feel sleepier than usual. Don't fight it. Climb into bed, put your feet up higher than your body and relax. Some women will tell you they slept through their pregnancies, a sign that extra rest is an accompanying condition. Eight to ten hours sleep at night and a nap during the day, if possible, should keep your energy level up.

Working

Generally, most women can work throughout most of their pregnancy. According to the American College of Obstetricians and Gynecologists (ACOG), a healthy woman with an uncomplicated pregnancy and a job posing no more hazards than those encountered in daily living may continue to work until the onset of labor. The final decision regarding work during pregnancy is up to you in consultation with your clinician.

If your job involves exposure to certain chemicals (see page 84), strenuous work, heavy lifting, long periods of time on your feet and/or unusually stressful conditions, you should request a transfer to a less stressful or hazardous work. Discuss this with your clinician and your employer. Your health, and that of your baby, must come first.

There are three major federal laws protecting the health, safety and employment rights of a pregnant employee:

1. *The Pregnancy Discrimination Act* requires employers to offer the same disability leave and pay to pregnant employees as they do for other employees who miss work for health related reasons. This Act makes it illegal to fire or refuse to promote a woman because she is pregnant. Should you feel you are being discriminated against because of your pregnancy call 1-800-669-3362.

2. *The Occupational Safety and Health Act (OSHA)* requires employers to reveal to their workers information regarding harmful agents in the workplace. This Act requires employers to provide a hazard-free workplace. If you believe your workplace is exposing you to hazardous agents and think it should be checked, call 1-800-356-4674.

3. *The Family and Medical Leave Act* requires employers with 50 or more employees to allow pregnant employees up to 12 weeks of unpaid leave during any 12 month period for the:

   - Birth, adoption or foster care of a child.

   - A serious health problem interfering with her ability to do her job due to a pregnancy, or birth-related disability.

   - The employee's need to take care of a spouse, a child, or a parent with a serious health problem.

For additional information about family and medical leave contact the Department of Labor at 1-800-959-3652

There are other decisions to make regarding work and your pregnancy. When should you tell your employer that you are pregnant? Many women wait until their third or fourth month of their pregnancy before telling their co-workers. This allows time for thinking over the situation and planning for changes both at work and at home. Once you are ready to discuss this at work, it is best to tell your boss first, rather than letting the gossip of co-workers carry the message in a way that could undermine your working relationship. If you run your own business, be sure to allow yourself enough time to find a replacement to manage things while you are away.

Should you tell your boss and co-workers whether you will return to work after the baby is born? Since they will certainly ask, it is probably best to put off making that decision until you have time to make long-range plans. If staying at home with your child is an option, do not make a commitment to others until you have decided for yourself.

Safety

The most important consideration if you continue working is safety on the job. Are conditions safe at work and conducive to good health for both you and your fetus?

Does your job involve pushing, lifting, pulling, or constant sitting or standing which may be hazardous or uncomfortable? Do you operate machinery that may become dangerous to run as your pregnancy progresses? Are you exposed to infectious diseases from working in a hospital or teaching small children? One important safety factor is your contact with certain chemicals. According to the American College of Obstetricians and Gynecologists, the following chemicals have been associated with hazards to the fetus or to the reproductive system of animals:

- Heavy metals: *cadmium, lead, mercury*
- Organic solvents: *benzene (benzol)*
- Hypoxic agents: *carbon monoxide*
- Anesthetic gases
- Halogenated gases
- Pesticides: *carbaryl, chlorinated hydrocarbons, chlordecone (kepone)*
- Miscellaneous: *carbon disulfide, ethylene oxide.*

Do you work with office machines that may use toxic substances? This is something that is often overlooked. Do you stand all day — which can lead to varicose veins, hemorrhoids, and fatigue?

Tell your clinician exactly what your job entails. If your job is deemed potentially dangerous to you during pregnancy perhaps you can work out an acceptable alternative, at least temporarily, so that you won't need to leave, be transferred, or lose seniority, benefits, or pay.

If you decide to quit your job or if you do not work outside the home, don't feel that your more flexible schedule permits you to disregard common sense. Any job, whether in the workplace or not requires setting priorities and providing time for rest and relaxation.

Exercise

Pregnant women should exercise. If you are healthy and your pregnancy is proceeding normally, there are a number of exercises you can do. Try to engage in some moderate form of exercise a minimum of 30 minutes every day. You need controlled exercises that will strengthen the muscles used during childbirth. Avoid activities that may lead to an accidental fall. Walking outdoors is healthful for everyone and you should make an effort to include a walk in your daily routine.

Ask your clinician about swimming, bowling, golf, or other sports you are accustomed to doing regularly. If you are used to the exercise, it doesn't bother you, and there are no unusual symptoms from the activity, you may continue within proper guidelines. The American College of Obstetricians and Gynecologists recommend the following:

- Do not exercise in hot, humid weather, or if you are ill with a fever.
- Do not allow your heart rate to exceed 140 beats per minute.
- Discontinue strenuous exercise after 15 minutes.
- Avoid jerky, bouncy, or jumping movements.
- Drink plenty of fluids to prevent dehydration.
- Stretch your muscles as you warm-up or cool down to avoid becoming sore and stiff.
- Do not stretch to the limit since hormone changes in pregnancy increase the looseness of the joints, so excessive stretching may lead to injury.
- After your first trimester, avoid exercises requiring you to be flat on your back for more than a few minutes.
- Avoid deep knee bends, sit-ups, raising both legs at once and straight leg toe touches.

Discontinue exercising and call your healthcare provider if any of the following symptoms occur:

- Pain
- Vaginal bleeding
- Shortness of breath
- Irregular or rapid heart rate
- Feeling faint or dizzy

Besides customary activities, the exercises shown in this book are recommended by the Maternity Center Association. In addition, some hospitals offer a series of prenatal exercise classes in an effort to make your labor easier and more efficient.

Some women have special circumstances requiring caution with regard to exercise. If you have heart disease or other chronic ailments, including high blood pressure, diabetes, anemia, or thyroid disease, you must modify your activity. Other women may not be able to exercise at all. For example, if you have a history of three or more miscarriages, multiple births, bleeding, placenta previa, incompetent cervix — or any such existing condition— you will probably not be permitted to exercise. If your clinician does give you the approval to proceed, remember to approach the exercises with common sense. Begin by doing one or two the first day, then build up gradually until you can do three to five of each every day. Never push yourself to the point of exhaustion or continue any exercise that hurts. The reasons for exercise are to help you relax, tone your muscles, and help condition your body for delivering your baby.

Yoga: Most forms of yoga during pregnancy are fine but avoid those exercises requiring you to lie flat on your back or over-stretching. Some yoga teachers offer special classes for pregnant women.

Kegel exercise: The pelvic floor muscles are one of the most important groups of muscles you should exercise. It is not uncommon for these muscles to relax late in the second or third trimester of pregnancy. The pelvic floor muscles form a figure 8 around the urethra, vagina and anus and will be very important when you deliver your baby.

Tailor sitting strengthens groin and leg area used during childbirth. Sit on the floor and bring your left foot toward you so it touches your body. Bring the right foot toward your left foot but do not cross your ankles. Lean forward slowly until your knees touch the floor. Sit this way, back straight, knees almost touching the floor, for a few minutes several times a day.

The backward stretch exercise helps strengthen the muscles of your back, pelvis and thighs. Begin by kneeling on your hands and knees keeping knees about 8 to 10 inches apart and your arms straight. Slowly curl backward, tucking your head toward your knees and keeping your arms extended as shown. Hold this position for a count of 5. Slowly come back up to original position on your hands and knees. Repeat this routine 5 times.

This exercise helps strengthen the muscles of your back and abdomen. Begin by kneeling on your hands and knees — your arms straight. Lift your left knee bringing it toward your elbow (straighten your leg without locking your knee). Now extend your leg up and back as shown. Move slowly — do not swing your leg back or arch your back. Follow the same movements with your right leg. Repeat 5 to 10 times with each leg.

Reaching and stretching for items on high shelves should be considered an exercise in controlled breathing. Before you stretch (not beyond your comfortable reach, of course) inhale, rise up on your toes and bring both arms upward at the same time. Then drop back on your heels and exhale slowly while returning your arms to your sides.

When you are working at a counter for a long period of time, bend your knees every little while and lean forward at the hips for a few minutes. This simple exercise is excellent for relieving backaches.

When you have to stand in one spot for a long time, place one foot forward and place all your weight on that foot for a few minutes. Then do the same with the other

There's an art to using a chair gracefully when you are pregnant. Use your leg muscles to lower yourself rather than "dropping" into the chair. To get up, slide to the front edge of the chair then push yourself up with your legs.

In Kegel exercises, you tighten the pelvic floor muscles the way you would to stop the flow of urine in midstream. The muscles will pull in together in the form of a figure 8, and the pelvic floor will lift slightly. You should hold these muscles tightly for two or three seconds and then release them. Kegel exercises should be repeated three to five times a day.

As your uterus grows it may put pressure on your bladder. As a result, stress urinary incontinence, the loss of urine when you cough, sneeze or laugh, is not unusual during pregnancy. Kegel exercises can help with this condition.

Travel

Seventy years ago, travel was a problem because cars and roads were less efficient and the bumps and jolts could cause problems. It was essential then to avoid long trips by car. Today, technology has made travel in cars, boats, planes, or trains fairly smooth and rapid so that there is little need to worry. Still, you should use common sense, and there are still a number of pre-cautions you should take. There are 7 basic guidelines you should follow when planning to travel:

1. When you take a trip some distance away, be sure to ask your clinician for the names of a reputable health care provider in the area in case of premature labor or miscarriage. Either problem can happen at home as well as away.

2. If you are taking a long trip by car, be sure to allow time for frequent stops so that you can drink a glass of water or juice, eat some nourishing food, stretch and urinate.

3. Whether you are a passenger or a driver, always wear the lap-shoulder belt throughout your pregnancy. There are some important guidelines for using seat belts while you are pregnant. Place the upper part of the belt between your breasts. Place the lower part of the lap-shoulder belt

under your abdomen as low as possible. Never place the lap belt above or across your abdomen. Keep the lower and upper belts snugly against you. If your car only has a lap belt, you should still use it—under your abdomen. Seat belts of any kind prevent damage and are much safer than no seat belt at all, so you should always use them.

4. If you cannot fit comfortably behind the wheel, it is best not to drive.

5. The current position of the American College of Obstetricians and Gynecologists (ACOG) on air travel is as follows: Any woman with an uncomplicated pregnancy can safely travel by air until 36 weeks gestation. Pregnant women at risk for preterm labor, pregnancy-induced high blood pressure, abnormalities of the placenta, uncontrolled diabetes or any other condition that could result in an unexpected emergency, should avoid air travel altogether. ACOG also recommends checking with the individual carrier to see if there are any specific requirements a pregnant woman should be aware of. International flights allow a pregnant woman to fly only until the 35th week of gestation. It is very important, particularly for a pregnant woman, to move about and stretch during the flight to help prevent blood clots.

6. You should consult with your clinician if you are planning to travel to a foreign country because of possible health risks. Some countries may have diseases that are not common in the United States. In certain areas the food or drinking water may have contaminents against which you have no built up resistance. Diarrhea, for example, is a common problem for a pregnant woman. Tell your clinician what country you are going to visit and discuss any possible health hazards that might arise. Also, do not worry about the metal detectors used for airport security because these detectors will not harm your fetus.

7. When you reach your ninth month of pregnancy, it is usually best to stay at home. It is not unusual for your baby to be born 2 weeks before or after your due date. Since that due date is uncertain, you will be most comfortable if you know you can quickly contact your own clinician and easily get to your local hospital.

Staying healthy

Treating a common cold during pregnancy may be a major chore. The virus seems to get a stronghold on pregnant women and hates to let go. You should be particularly cautious about avoiding chills and large crowds of people during cold and flu season. If you catch a cold consult your clinician about medication. Do not treat yourself with any over-the-counter medications. Almost all drugs taken by the mother cross the placenta to the fetus and must be used with caution.

Dental check-up

Scientific studies have shown that there is a relationship between pregnancy and dental decay, also called "caries." Pregnancy can affect the condition of the teeth and gums. Any untreated dental problem is more likely to get worse. Bleeding gums, possibly leading to an infection, can also occur during pregnancy. Using a softer toothbrush may help control or minimize the bleeding. Recent evidence links poor dental hygiene and associated disease with a risk of preterm labor.

It is a good idea to visit your dentist early in your pregnancy and follow his or her recommendations. A complete dental checkup early in your pregnancy can likely save you from toothaches later. If you need an extraction, the dentist can use a local anesthetic. Be sure to tell your dentist you are pregnant so special precautions can be taken if your teeth require an X-ray.

Following your dentist's recommendations is essential. The American Dental Association issues special brochures about the importance of dental care during pregnancy. Your teeth and gums can be strengthened by improving your eating habits and getting sufficient vitamins and calcium. It is your responsibility to conscientiously brush your teeth each morning, each night, and if at all possible, after each meal. Rinsing your mouth once or twice a day, and the proper use of dental floss, will help eliminate decay-causing bacteria.

*D*RUGS OF ALL TYPES ARE AVAILABLE TODAY AS EFFECTIVE remedies for a variety of ailments. Both prescription and over-the-counter drugs are so prevalent in our modern society that we often look to them as if they were the answers to all our health problems.

The cardinal rule for every pregnant woman is that no drug can be assumed harmless when you are expecting.

If you become pregnant and are taking medication prescribed for a preexisting medical conditions such as diabetes, hypertension, epilepsy or heart disease don't stop your medication without discussing it with your clinician. Once aware of your pregnancy, he or she may prescribe another medication or modify your current dosage.

In this chapter we'll examine chemicals and hazards that seem so ordinary yet can be very threatening to the expectant mother.

Teratogens: These are agents that can cause structural damage to the fetus when a woman is exposed to them during pregnancy. These agents can be drugs or chemicals in the environment, at home or in the work place.

Herbal supplements

Some herbal products claim to treat pregnancy-related discomforts. Since herbs come from plants and are all-natural, many people believe they must be safe. This is not necessarily true. Today, there are estimated to be over 400 herbs in common use. Some of these herbal preparations are known to be toxic, and on rare occasions fatal. Herbal medicines pose special risks to pregnant women and their fetuses. Unlike conventional drugs, herbal preparations are not tested or regulated by the FDA. Manufacturers of herbal products are not required by law to conduct studies demonstrating their safety and effectiveness. Because of this, there are no standard quality controls over these preparations. The result is that the composition of an herbal supplement can vary from one batch to the next.

There are currently no scientific studies to back up the claims some promoters make about herbs improving the milk supply of lactating women. In fact, there are some herbs that when taken by a pregnant woman or breastfeeding mother can cause problems. For example, the herb comfrey has been shown to cause liver failure, particularly in infants and should not be used by nursing mothers. Comfrey is illegal in Canada*. A number of them are also known to interact with certain drugs.

An article appearing in the April 2003 issue of *OB-Gyn News,* specifically cited goldenseal, black cohosh and ephedra as herbal supplements which should not be used during pregnancy. An article appearing in the August 2004 issue of *Ob-Gyn News,* indicated that blue cohosh should be avoided entirely in pregnancy. Blue cohosh is often used in combination with black cohosh as a uterine tonic. Both have been known to cause complications in the fetus.

If you have any questions about specific herbal supplements call Motherisk at (416) 813-6780 or go to the website: www.motherisk.org.

Common drugs

If you are pregnant make your healthcare provider aware of your pregnancy. You should not take any pill, capsule, powder, or liquid medicine unless your clinician prescribes it. That includes over-the-counter remedies such as aspirin, laxatives, cough and cold medicines, nose drops, external ointments, vitamins, antacids, tranquilizers, and sedatives. A common drug or household remedy may be safe under ordinary circumstances but dangerous to the pregnant woman or her fetus. Consult your clinician before taking any medicines since he or she knows about you and your pregnancy.

Aspirin: According to the American College of Obstetricians and Gynecologists (ACOG), there are differing conclusions about the role of

*In the United States, the Food and Drug Administration recently sent out a warning letter to supplement manufacturers stating comfrey poses a serious health threat and should not be used as a dietary supplement.

aspirin in causing birth defects. Research has proven
that taking aspirin during pregnancy can change
clotting factors in the blood of both the mother
and the fetus. Aspirin may also affect certain
aspects of the fetal circulation system. Because
it may be potentially dangerous during pregnancy, ACOG recommends that expectant mothers
should not take aspirin except under supervision
of their healthcare providers.

As an alternative for relieving a headache, try
taking a nap with a cold cloth covering your
eyes or go for a walk. If these aren't helpful ask

Unless specifically ordered by your physician

your doctor for other recommendations. Most clinicians will allow you to take
Tylenol®. It is best to check with your provider.

Other over-the-counter drugs: You'll need to read the labels of over-the-counter drugs such as pain relievers, cold remedies, sinus medicine and sedatives,
most of which contain aspirin. Look for the words "acetylsalicylic acid" or
"acetylsalicylate". These are scientific terms for aspirin, and they often appear
on labels of other medications. Two other ingredients that are related to aspirin
and should also be avoided are salicylates and salicylamides.

The FDA has issued a warning that the ingredient phenylpropanolamine
(PPA) found in some pain relievers, cold medications, appetite suppressants,
sedatives and sinus medications should not be taken by anyone. Check your
medicine cabinet. If you have any medication containing PPA discard it.
Read labels on all over-the-counter remedies carefully. If you feel you must
have relief from your cold symptoms, think twice and, above all, check with
your clinician.

There are many other nonprescription medications that have not been studied extensively and so it is not known if they can damage a fetus. It is wise
to refrain from using any drug when little or no information about its effect are
known.

Accutane® (Isotretinoin): Used to treat severe acne, Accutane may cause birth
defects and should not be used during pregnancy or for the month prior to

becoming pregnant. Retin A, which is molecularly similar to Accutane, may also present a risk of birth defects and should not be used in pregnancy.

The Food and Drug Administration (FDA) and the manufacturer of the drug Accutane, developed a system to manage Accutane-related teratogenicity (changes during the development of a fetus), known as SMART. SMART is designed to strengthen the existing pregnancy prevention program. The FDA recommends the pregnancy prevention program require documentation of a negative pregnancy test be given to the pharmacy before a prescription for Accutane can be filled. An FDA advisory panel is now recommending even more restrictions to help reduce exposure of the fetus to this drug.

Other drugs

In the early 1960's a drug called Thalidomide was used as an effective sedative that also relieved morning sickness. It had been tested in animals and was thought to be safe. However, it was discovered later that animals were not nearly as susceptible to the effects of thalidomide as were human fetuses. The result of thalidomide's widespread use by pregnant women was an increase in the number of children born with arm and leg deformities.

In a similar manner, the drug DES (diethylstilbestrol) was given to women in the 1950's to prevent miscarriage. In the 1970's, an increased incidence of vaginal cancer was found among adolescent girls whose mothers had taken DES during their pregnancies.

Both of these drugs were considered safe when they were first used, yet proved to have tragic human consequences. That is why women should carefully consider taking any prescription or over-the-counter medication when pregnant.

Two studies reported in the British medical journal, *Lancet,* indicated that males who were exposed to the drug phenobarbital before birth had long-term lower intelligence test scores. Exposure to this drug in late pregnancy had an even more profound effect.

Marijuana, cocaine, and other mind-altering drugs: If you are using any mind-altering drugs, such as marijuana, cocaine or LSD, stop immediately. Common sense should tell you that using any of these drugs jeopardizes not only your health but also the health of your unborn child.

Studies have shown that women who use cocaine may have a higher rate of spontaneous abortion than women who do not use the drug. Infants born to mothers who used cocaine during their pregnancies are more likely to have neurological and behavior problems, seizures and sudden infant death syndrome (SIDS) than are babies born to mothers who did not use the drug during their pregnancies. If a fetus is exposed to cocaine it may have a greater risk of birth defects and even death at or around the time of birth.

Researchers at the National Association for Prenatal Addiction Research and Education (NAPARE) tested 3-year-olds whose mothers used cocaine with alcohol, marijuana and tobacco during pregnancy, and found there was a direct effect on intelligence. The study indicates that children exposed to cocaine and other drugs prior to birth scored lower on intelligence tests. The level of development depends also on other factors such as individual behavioral characteristics and quality of home environment. Because they are mind-altering drugs, most healthcare providers also feel the effect of these drugs prevents the expectant mother from being fully attentive during her pregnancy and afterwards to the needs of her baby.

Finally, research has established that babies born to women addicted to narcotics are themselves addicted at birth and may die from unrecognized withdrawal symptoms.

Alcohol

Alcohol is a drug. Although it was once thought that moderate drinking did not threaten the fetus, it is now acknowledged that alcohol can have devastating effects on the unborn child. Clinicians agree there is no minimum level of alcohol a pregnant woman can drink and be certain the fetus is not harmed. Studies also indicate that even moderate drinking increases the risk of miscarriage.

In 1968 in France and again in 1972 in the United States, doctors noted a similar pattern of features in children born to alcoholic women. These children were characterized by poor growth both before and after birth, as well as structural changes such as abnormalities of the face, ears, joints, limbs and heart, and mental retardation. This clearly indicates that the damage occurs while the tissues of the fetus are developing. The term "fetal alcohol syndrome" (FAS) is given to these children whose mother's levels of alcohol during pregnancy affected their fetus.

The impact of alcohol on the fetus increases with the level of exposure. Some mothers may be more susceptible than others to the adverse effects of alcohol or its breakdown products. Smoking, drug abuse, and malnutrition complicate the picture further. No alcoholic beverages should be consumed during pregnancy. According to an article published in the December 1, 2001 issue of the *OB-GYN News* there is no known "safe" amount of alcohol exposure to the fetus.

Scientists are searching for the reason why alcohol is so damaging to the unborn. So far the studies are inconclusive except for the fact that alcohol affects the brain of the fetus. The effects of alcohol on the fetus remain after the birth even though the alcohol has been removed.

For most pregnant women the question of alcohol revolves around social drinking. The best answer, of course, is to treat alcohol as you would any other drug and not use it. When attending social gatherings drink non-alcoholic beverages. You wouldn't give a gin and tonic to your newborn, so why offer it to your unborn baby?

The problem of alcohol can also be related to the father. Published results from a 12 year study[1] indicate that if a man consumes alcohol prior to mating there can be fetal abnormalities even if the woman does not drink any alcohol. These studies suggest that alcohol can also have a mutagenic (an abnormal change in the genes) effect on the sperm. One of the interesting points in the study was that these damaging effects are found primarily among the moderate drinkers rather than the very heavy drinkers. The reason being, that a large intake of alcohol frequently causes male infertility.

A report of a study published in the April, 1993 issue of *OB-GYN News,* indicated that it was the frequency of alcohol use by the father that was important, and that daily intake of an alcoholic beverage was associated with a

---

[1] *Rush-Presbyterian-St. Luke's Medical Center, Insights into clinical and scientific progress in medicine.1991. Vol. 14, No. 2, page 34*

reduction in the birth weight by 45 grams (1.6 ounces) at full term delivery (40 weeks gestation).

Caffeine

If you stop drinking alcohol and switch to coffee or tea, you should know that coffee and tea are stimulants for both you and your fetus. Exposing the developing fetus to high amounts of caffeine may have harmful effects. Caffeine has strong chemical effects on the human body and is known to cross the placenta.

An article in the June 1, 1998 issue of *OB-GYN News,* reported an association between sudden infant death syndrome (SIDS) and caffeine in women who consumed large amounts of caffeine per day. The equivalent of 14 cups of tea, 7 cups of coffee or 12-15 glasses of cola.

Since the human risk factors are not conclusively known, moderate use or elimination of caffeine during pregnancy would be prudent advice. Decaffeinated coffee, fruit juices and non-cola drinks can be substituted. Cutting back on tea is also beneficial because tea interferes with iron absorption. Take the time to check product labels carefully for items containing caffeine.

Some herbal teas may be harmful. Since little is known about the effects of herbal teas on pregnancy it is best to avoid them. Labeling a product as "natural" does not mean it is safe. The herb comfrey is known to cause serious liver disease. Another herb known to be harmful is blue cohosh (see pages 92-93).

Smoking

There is no reason for you to smoke even if you were not pregnant. Your pregnancy is an excellent reason for you to quit. Smoking is not only a known health risk for you, but it can affect your fetus in a number of ways. Tobacco smoke is a major source of carbon monoxide which can interfere with the amount of oxygen your fetus receives. Carbon monoxide is also found in the exhaust fumes from automobiles. Consequently, if you are pregnant, you should avoid waiting in long gas lines or in traffic jams where cars are idling their engines.

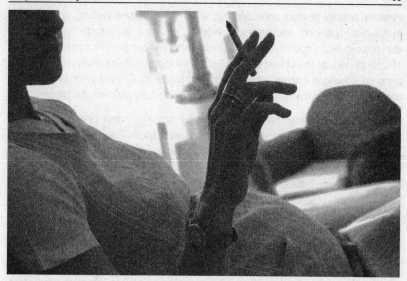

Studies have shown that newborns whose mothers smoked have an increased incidence of birth defects and a higher risk of sudden infant death syndrome (SIDS). A study in Sweden found that mothers who smoked during pregnancy were more likely to give birth to babies with limb-reduction malformations. These risks increase in proportion to the number of cigarettes you smoke each day.

Researchers have also discovered that smoking can result in miscarriage, smaller babies, and premature births. A pregnant woman who smokes heavily may increase the chances of premature birth as much as 2½ times the rate for nonsmokers. Your smoking could make the difference if you have had repeated miscarriages or premature labor. A low birth weight can threaten the health of a baby, maybe even threaten its life, and smokers tend to have smaller babies.

Smoking during pregnancy can be an additional risk factor for very low birth weight (VLBW). According to studies, VLBW children whose mothers smoked during pregnancy were more likely to have an IQ score below 85. This is another good reason to give up smoking.

Passive smoke is also implicated in small-for-gestation babies and genetic mutations. Not only are pregnant women advised not to smoke, but they should also avoid spending time in places where other people smoke. A group of researchers at the University of Minnesota found evidence of nicotine in the urine of newborn babies whose mothers smoked. Researchers believe this proves nicotine, a known cancer-causing substance, crosses the placenta.

Morning sickness can be complicated by smoking, and pregnant women often find smoking irritating. The American Cancer Society has designed programs to help pregnant women "kick" the smoking habit. For more information, call your local American Cancer Society office. For more information on how smoking affects your baby, see page 160.

Necessary drugs

Recognizing the dangers of certain drugs and avoiding them during pregnancy is important. However, in certain situations, drugs are necessary and sometimes vital for the health of both the mother and the fetus.

If a pregnant woman requires surgery, develops a severe infection, or suffers an injury, she would need some drugs for her treatment. In fact, not using drugs in those situations might be disastrous. Similarly, women with chronic diseases such as high blood pressure, diabetes or epilepsy may have to use drugs on a routine basis. If a woman finds herself in a life-threatening situation, drug therapy may be the only answer.

The key to using these necessary drugs wisely is to remember the risk but consider the alternative. Often, dosages can be changed, or a drug that is equally effective but less powerful can be substituted. The clinician will evaluate the pregnant woman who needs drugs and monitor her usage. This close relationship with the clinician is the best way for a pregnant woman to minimize the risks while at the same time regaining or maintaining her own health.

Vaccines are another example of necessary drug usage for the expectant mother. Some vaccines, such as immunizations against diphtheria, tetanus and hepatitis, are permissible if the mother has not already been vaccinated or is in some risk of contagion. These vaccines should not be administered, though, until the second or third trimester of pregnancy. In contrast, live vaccines, such as those for rubella, measles or mumps, should not be given during pregnancy.

Statistics show that your chances for having a healthy baby are good, and you can handle most problems without endangering your baby's health. If you are taking any medication prescribed by your clinician, be sure he or she knows if you are trying to conceive. If you become pregnant, your clinician should be notified promptly.

Household substances

In today's world there has been a significant increase in the chemicals that we use in our homes. There are parts of our environment that we cannot control, but we should try to be aware of these chemicals in our own homes and avoid unnecessary exposure.

Paint and paint fumes, especially from oil-based paint and turpentine, should be avoided by pregnant women. There is no evidence that these petroleum products cause harm, but there is also no proof that they do not. So it is best to let someone else paint the nursery. If you must help, stay off the ladder and keep the room well ventilated. The fumes could lead to dizziness and a fall.

Another household job that you should avoid is spraying the house or garden with insecticides or herbicides. These chemicals are potentially dangerous, and some can be absorbed through the skin. Give another family member the task of spraying insects and weeds.

A third category of household chemicals you should handle with care is cleaning products. Many cleaning products have strong chemicals that can be absorbed through the skin. You can use these products safely if you take the proper precautions.

Vaccines

Safe to take during pregnancy

- Diphtheria
- Tetanus

Not routinely given but are safe to use if you may come in contact with disease

- Hepatitis B
- Pneumonia
- Rabies
- Influenza
- Polio

Not to be given during pregnancy

- Measles
- Rubella
- Mumps
- Varicella-zoster (Chickenpox)
- Any vaccine using live viruses

It is also a good idea to find substitutes whenever possible for aerosol sprays. The reason is that their mist can enter your lungs. So far, not much is known about the danger of these chemicals, but there is no point in taking this risk. Fortunately, mechanical pump containers have replaced many aerosol cans making it easier to find a suitable product for you needs.

Environmental substances

Our environment contains a variety of chemicals and you can take some precautions against them. Air pollution caused by auto exhaust fumes should be avoided. In some communities the sanitation systems may not treat agricultural chemicals in the water. You can compensate by installing a filter on the tap that you use for drinking water, or buying bottled water. Some building materials contain formaldehyde or asbestos and should be avoided. When buying produce, it is best to select products that have not been sprayed with agricultural insecticide or fertilizer. Since you may not know what chemicals were sprayed on them, it is best to wash all fruits and vegetables thoroughly.

Toxoplasmosis

Toxoplasmosis is caused by a one-celled organism called Toxoplasma. This organism may exist in cats and some food animals such as pigs, sheep and cattle. The organism causes a minor infection of the blood and other organs in human beings. Because it is such a mild disease, its victim usually does not notice it.

Toxoplasmosis can seriously damage a fetus. About one third of the babies born to mothers infected during their pregnancies are also infected at birth. These babies may be born prematurely, have a low birth weight, be jaundiced, have eye problems, and suffer from other long-range complications.

Therefore, precautions must be taken if you are a cat owner. Cats acquire the parasite by eating rats or mice which carry the parasite eggs. The parasite lodges in the cat's intestinal tract and completes a full life cycle, making new larvae. You may feel safe because you think that your cat doesn't eat rodents, but it is difficult to be sure if your cat spends any time outdoors.

Consequently, it is always best to be on the safe side to protect yourself and your baby. You do not have to get rid of the cat. You just need to take the following precautions:

- Do not empty or clean the cat's litter box. Let someone else handle that chore. The reason is that the parasite's eggs are passed from the cat's intestinal tract into its feces.

- Changing the litter every day will prevent the parasite eggs from becoming infective during the first 24 hours after they are passed.

- Whenever you handle the cat or any of its belongings, wash your hands thoroughly.

- Wear gloves when gardening.

- Avoid stray cats.

If you own a dog, you do not need to worry about toxoplasmosis. This parasite does not use dogs as a host. In fact, we do not know of any other disease carried by dogs that is dangerous to pregnant women. If you do not own a cat, there are still some precautions you should take because toxoplasma eggs are carried by some food animals which pick up the eggs from the soil and grasses that they eat. The most common offenders are lamb and pork, but beef cattle can be infected as well. All of your meat should be well cooked in order to be completely free of toxoplasmosis. Heat kills this organism. You should also wash your hands thoroughly after handling raw meat when preparing meals.

Radiation

Radiation used in the X-ray of internal organs is called ionizing radiation. Pregnant women who work around ionizing radiation should wear protective clothing or shields against exposure to this radiation. Much larger doses of ionizing radiation used in the treatment of cancer for example, can harm the fetus.

The radiation from color television sets, video display screens and microwave ovens known as non-ionizing radiation, is not thought to be at dangerous levels. According to the Oregon Occupational Safety and Health Division of OSHA, there is not enough evidence available to support the position that exposure to video display terminals (VDT) electromagnetic fields may cause birth defects and miscarriages. A study by the National Institute for Occupational Safety and Health and the American Cancer Society found no increase in the risk of miscarriage associated with occupational use of VDTs. Their conclusion was that "VDT use alone is not a hazard to the pregnant worker, but that poor work postures and job stresses often associated with prolonged or intense work are hazards." Other studies have shown that the bulk of the evidence "thus far indicates that VDTs in themselves do not increase the risk for adverse pregnancy outcome." This finding was reported by the U.S. Department of Health and Human Services in September 1999.

The abused woman

Physical, sexual or emotional abuse is, sadly, one of the most common health problems in America. It frequently begins, or gets worse during pregnancy, putting both the mother and fetus at risk.

Abuse is wrong! No one has a legal right to do this to you. If you are being abused you must let someone know immediately. Speak to your clinician, nurse, clergyman, counselor, or close friend. Get in touch with a crisis center in your area. There are legal aid services, domestic violence programs and shelters available for battered women and children. If you or your children are in physical danger have a fast exit plan for an emergency.

National Domestic Violence Hotline: (800) 799-SAFE / (800) 787-3224

National Child Abuse Hotline: (800) 422-4453

Conclusion

Some people think that a fetus is safely sheltered inside its mother, away from the toxic environment outside, but this is not entirely true. This chapter examined how drugs and other substances can pass from the outside environment to the mother and subsequently to the fetus. This information is not meant to frighten you. It is provided to make you aware of what can help as well as harm your fetus as it develops. The rule of moderation operates in regard to drugs. If you combine common sense with the information in this chapter about drugs, your fetus will grow and develop properly. Be assured that statistics continue to show most babies will be born normal and healthy.

Chapter 9 Your appearance

NOW THAT YOU ARE PREGNANT you will likely be even more aware and conscientious about your personal appearance. For reasons of both comfort and hygiene, changes in your bathing routine, hairstyle, cosmetics, and wardrobe can help improve your overall sense of well-being during pregnancy.

In an earlier chapter, we discussed the fact that your body is excreting waste material for the fetus as well as for yourself. As a result, your pregnancy has increased both the frequency of urination and amount of urine you are excreting. Trips to the bathroom will be more frequent, and the pressure of the fetus on your bladder may cause some occasional leakage when laughing or moving around.

Adapting your grooming routine to the changes you are experiencing will insure that you both maintain your appearance and stay comfortable throughout your pregnancy.

Bathing

You can assure a feeling of freshness by taking a daily shower or bath, whichever you prefer. Bathing can have many benefits. A daily bath will wash away accumulated wastes that may lodge in the enlarged pores of your skin. And, a warm bath can be very relaxing, though there are a few precautions you should take. As your abdomen gets larger and heavier, you may need assistance getting into and out of the tub. To prevent falls use a non-slip mat on the floor. Tub baths are not harmful even at the end of your pregnancy, but you do need to limit the temperature of your bath water.

There have been several studies indicating that hot baths, saunas, hot tubs, and sitz baths during the first 3 months of a pregnancy may increase the risk of birth defects. Lukewarm baths are permissible. A study of 23,000 women who had heat exposure from a sauna, hot tub or a fever during the first three months of their pregnancies supports the theory that heat is a teratogen, an agent that can cause birth defects when a woman is exposed to it during her pregnancy.

If you have a vaginal discharge, mild soap and water is all you need to cleanse yourself. Douching, vaginal deodorants and sprays should be avoided during pregnancy.

Be aware also that during pregnancy your nipples may become caked from a discharge of colostrum. They should be washed gently with soft cotton and warm water without using soap. Avoid stimulating the nipples by gently patting, not rubbing them dry.

Your skin

During pregnancy, your skin may undergo a variety of changes. You can easily adapt your grooming routine to accommodate the changes you are experiencing and to maintain your appearance and comfort throughout your pregnancy. If your skin becomes drier it may need lubrication to smooth and soften it. For this, use a liquid moisturizer. Always applying it before your makeup. Dark circles may occur around your eyes, especially if you are a brunette. These circles will eventually disappear. In the meantime, you can cover them with foundation. If your skin color becomes too rosy due to the increased circulation of blood, you can tone it down by using a soft, translucent shade of powder.

Chloasma is the name for brownish blotches that appear around the eyes and nose. These will disappear or fade after delivery when hormone levels return to normal. You may notice that skin changes seem to increase with exposure to sunlight.

During pregnancy red spots may appear on your body. These are called angiomas. Some women will see a reddish color on the palms of their hands. This is Palmer erythema. Both of these conditions are caused by the high level of estrogen in the body and will disappear after delivery.

There are a number of skin products you must avoid while you are pregnant. Do not use wrinkle creams containing Retin A or Renova since both contain vitamin A. Vitamin A is important to good health but may be responsible for birth defects when taken in large amounts during pregnancy.

There is one type of rash that occurs only in pregnant women called pruritic urticarial papules of pregnancy or PUPP. This rash can cause severe itching. PUPP is characterized by hives or red patches appearing first in the stretch marks on the abdomen. The rash can then spread to the arms, legs and back. Fortunately, it almost never spreads to the face.

PUPP is more common during a first pregnancy and in women having twins. This condition usually occurs late in the pregnancy and poses no risk to the fetus. The only sure way to make it disappear is to deliver your baby. If you are still many weeks away from your due date, ask your healthcare professional to recommend something to relieve the itching.

Hair removal from your legs can also irritate dry skin, but you can compensate by shaving with a lotion instead of soap lather, and moisturizing the area afterwards. Avoid hair removal creams (depilatories) containing chemicals that have not been extensively studied. Waxing unwanted hair is safe.

Occasionally, over-active glands may cause a skin condition that resembles acne. The best solution for this is regular washings with warm, sudsy water. The drug Accutane used to treat severe acne must not be used during pregnancy because it has been linked to birth defects.

Many women notice another change in their skin called the linea nigra. This is a darkening of a line running from the top of the abdomen to the bottom. As your pregnancy progresses, other streaks or stretch marks may appear on your abdomen or breasts. You cannot prevent these stretch marks, but they will slowly fade after your delivery.

Your hair

There are several possible changes that may occur to your hair during pregnancy. Hormone changes and glandular secretions may cause your hair to become oilier or drier. You may need to wash your hair more often than before you became pregnant. Changing shampoos or hair dressing to recondition your hair may help.

One problem that some women have is a loss of hair. If your hair does start to thin out, you should avoid processes such as permanents, straightening, or coloring. All of these use chemicals that can damage thin or dry hair. The safety of hair dyes on the fetus has not yet been determined conclusively. For this reason many women postpone coloring their hair until after their pregnancies. Should you decide to permanent your hair, keep in mind the solution used contains ammonia. To ensure your own safety, be certain you are in a well-ventilated area when applying the solution to your hair.

Clothing

Today's mother-to-be is fortunate to have a wide variety of fashions available to choose from. You can find clothes that will allow you to dress for every occasion in comfort and style. Designers have become more and more aware that they need to offer women maternity fashions that are attractive and inexpensive. You will probably feel the need for larger clothes about the middle of the 4th month of pregnancy.

A wide variety of maternity clothes are available in department stores. In addition, you will find many maternity fashions in mail order catalogs and online. If you enjoy styling and sewing your own clothes, and have the time, there are patterns available that can be assembled quickly and inexpensively. Or you could take some of your existing clothes and tailor them.

Your choice of clothes really depends on your life style, whether you stay at home or work elsewhere, whether you socialize and entertain with friends or prefer to relax at home. Generally you will need only a few new outfits that you can accent with accessories you already own. Any new accessories that you buy can become a part of your regular wardrobe in the future.

Another sensible alternative for your wardrobe is the inclusion of separates. By mixing and matching a variety of colorful blouses, you can recycle a pair of slacks and a skirt many times. There is also a wide selection of sports outfits, bathing suits, and lounging apparel.

Most women now prefer to wear pantihose. There are two styles of maternity pantihose available, support maternity pantihose and regular sheer maternity pantihose. Regular queen-size pantihose (for larger, not taller figures) are less expensive than maternity pantihose.

Underpants should be larger than your normal size so that they don't bind or cause irritation. A cotton crotch is preferred because it is more absorbent and also because it allows air to flow to the genital area. You will have to wash these garments numerous times, so it's best to choose more durable, less glamorous designs rather than frilly, fragile lingerie.

As your breasts enlarge, you can either buy a maternity bra or a regular bra in a larger size. Maternity bras are specially designed to give more support than ordinary bras, and most women find them more comfortable. You will have to decide what type you prefer and decide when you feel you need one, based on the size, heaviness and discomfort of your breasts. When you get to the later stages of your pregnancy, you may want to select a nursing bra which has panels on the cup that unhook for easy breastfeeding. Some clinicians recommend that you wear a bra at all times.

Flat-heeled or low, broad-heeled shoes are the most sensible for the pregnant woman. As your abdomen becomes larger, your center of equilibrium changes. There should be no major problems adjusting to this change, but you may not be able to move as gracefully, quickly or with the same surefootedness as before. You'll find high heels are impractical from the point of view of both safety and comfort. They tend to thrust the abdomen forward and create a swayback posture, possibly resulting in backaches and leg cramps. Clinicians recommend avoiding footwear that lifts your heels 3 to 4 inches off the ground pushing your weight forward so that it must be supported by the balls of your feet and your toes.

Chapter 10 Fatherhood

*F*OR A LONG TIME, CHILDBIRTH HAD BEEN VIEWED from a narrow perspective in which everyone involved was thought to be excited and happy. Recently, however, a study by two prominent sociologists discovered that having a child may lead to a serious crisis in a marriage. The question is why this occurs?

One reason is that having a child can threaten the balance of responsibility and compatibility in a marriage. For example, if both young parents have been working, the new child can mean additional expenses for only one income. Also, a woman who enjoys her work and the time spent with adults may now find that her new responsibilities are stifling and boring. The woman may understand that she has to give up many aspects of her former lifestyle, but she may be resentful. Even though her interest in the many aspects of her pregnancy is there, she may still become temperamental and irritable.

Sometimes, the woman can make the mistake of shutting the husband out because she feels that she is the only one involved in the childbirth. One husband who faced such a situation spoke for many others when he said, "Karen has been so wrapped up in having a baby for so long that sometimes I feel as though she has forgotten about me." Such an example can help the woman to remember that childbirth is a family affair, and that the father should not be left out. What can be done to make sure that the father is involved and feels important?

Sharing the pregnancy

One of the changes taking place in the pregnant woman is the increased production of certain hormones needed for motherhood. These hormone changes affect your brain as well as your body, and they help to prepare you psychologically for an innate maternal feeling. While these changes are occurring within your delicate system, no such changes are taking place inside the father. In fact, the father often does not grasp the feeling of being a parent until he finally holds the new child in his arms.

It is important to help the father gradually share the experience of pregnancy. Have the father talk with your clinician as soon as you learn that you are pregnant. Clinicians prefer to have both of the prospective parents involved and informed. Share this book with him so he'll be able to understand all of the changes, both physical and emotional, that are occurring within you. After reading this, the father will be more understanding when you complain about a backache, or leg pains. He will also know that these conditions are normal. Encourage your partner to put his hand on your abdomen so that he can feel the baby's movement and share the experience. Consult with him when selecting the baby's furnishings and planning the routine for your new baby. Finally, remember that while so much of your time and energy is being spent planning for the baby you can't forget to make time for each other. You are both under more than the usual amount of stress at this time, so it is especially important that both of you are more understanding and thoughtful of each other, and that you set aside quality time to spend together.

Sexual relations

There is so much misinformation about sexual intercourse during pregnancy that clinicians often marvel at the highly imaginative questions their patients ask. Because sex is an important part of your life, an objective look at the facts will help.

During a normal pregnancy, sexual relations are not harmful. If there is no bleeding and your membranes have not ruptured, intercourse anytime during your pregnancy is desirable, permissible and safe. The rule of moderation should also be followed.

There are no rules concerning frequency of sexual intercourse. Simply consider your own physical desires and use mature judgement. Interestingly, it has been recognized that some women experience heightened sexual desire during pregnancy because of the increase in their female hormones. Having an orgasm is not harmful in any way, and in fact, knowing that you do not have to fear becoming pregnant tends to increase the sexual enjoyment.

Of course, the woman's body is changing shape, so some adjustments may be required from your normal habits. Pregnancy can even be a good time to experiment with new sexual positions. The changes in the woman's shape during pregnancy can make the position in which the male is above the female awkward or uncomfortable. If so, you may find it more comfortable for the female to assume the position above the male. Other positions can

be tried to satisfy individual needs. If vaginal discomfort occurs due to lack of lubrication, try applying a lotion, jelly or cream to the genital area, but be sure to check with your clinician first.

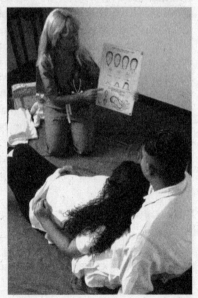

More than ever before, it is important for both parents to remain faithful to each other in a monogamous relationship. During pregnancy there are greater risks involved with sexually transmitted diseases. Such diseases can be dangerous to both the mother and the fetus (see pages 5-7). Beyond these simple guidelines, any further questions about the practice of sexual activities should be discussed with your clinician. Have an open, candid discussion with him or her. In the last four weeks of pregnancy, it may be desirable to limit some sexual relations, but only rarely is it necessary to completely abstain from sex at any time during the pregnancy.

Fathers in the labor and delivery room

There are arguments for each side on whether the prospective father should accompany his partner throughout labor and delivery. While some hospitals permit it, others do not. Your clinician will be able to tell you whether this is possible, practical and, depending on your personal situation, recommended. Usually if a hospital allows the father into the delivery room, he may be required to attend classes for new parents.

Classes for father

Classes for first-time fathers are sponsored by many civic organizations including your hospital, the local Red Cross, the YMCA or Maternal Health Centers. To find such programs, you should ask your clinician, call your hospital, or look in the phone book for the appropriate organization. The classes usually focus on giving practical advice concerning the father's role during pregnancy. They also show the father how to help with the new baby.

Men are also able to reassure one another during these classes, and most sessions include both the prospective father and the mother. If you take the classes together, you'll not only have fun as a couple, but also build a solid basis of shared companionship for your adventure ahead.

Chapter 11 Planning ahead

*P*LANNING FOR YOUR NEW BABY'S FUTURE is a fun and exciting part of the new adventure ahead of you. Preparing yourself for your baby's birth, and understanding how to care for and nourish your child before his or her arrival, will give you confidence as your new life as a family begins.

Prepared childbirth

For the general public, this has become one of the most interesting aspects of childbirth. Still, there are many people who are confused by the term prepared childbirth and have misconceptions regarding exactly what it means.

In prepared childbirth, the pregnant woman strives to deliver her baby using the natural function of labor. She can and does take advantage of modern facilities, and there is complete medical supervision. Whether medication and instruments are used depends on the mother's progress during delivery. If a woman would like to have her baby naturally and without anesthesia, she needs to take childbirth classes to prepare her both psychologically and physically. In prepared childbirth, the clinician is at the woman's side to supervise and guide, direct the progress of labor, and manage any situation that may arise. Prepared childbirth stresses that the team around the woman — the father or attending coach, the clinician, and the nurse — assist and encourage her.

The idea behind natural childbirth and the appeal it has for mothers are the same — safety for the baby and satisfaction for the mother. The main advantage for the clinician is also increased safety because fewer drugs are needed. Safety for the baby is always the prime consideration for the mother. Another important consideration for her is that she will enjoy the experience more if she has learned and practiced the routine and knows what she is doing.

You do not have to decide right away whether you prefer this type of delivery, but you should consider it. You can even get a better idea of what it is all about by attending some prepared childbirth classes. Your pregnancy will be unique to you, so your needs and reactions may change as your pregnancy progresses. You can discuss the types of delivery with your clinician sometime during the second trimester. Regardless of your decision, in the delivery room you must be prepared to let your clinician decide on the proper procedures. He or she will determine the best and most appropriate course of action for you and your baby.

Breastfeeding

Almost any woman who decides to breastfeed her baby is able to do so. Breast or nipple size or shape does not affect a mother's ability to nurse her baby. Most women today consider breastfeeding even if only for a short time.

Breast milk is a perfect baby food because it has all the necessary food elements in just the right proportions necessary for healthy development.

Breast milk offers immunological protection. The substance found in colostrum, the milky or yellowish fluid secreted by the mammary glands a few days before and after birth, as well as in the mature milk, protects your baby against a number of infections. The colostrum also acts as a laxative, helping clear the baby's body of mucus and meconium, a black stool which builds up during the last months of pregnancy. Colostrum also contains growth factors and hormones that can stimulate cell growth.

It is therefore beneficial to your baby to breastfeed if even for only a short period of time. There are other benefits of breastfeeding as well:

- Breastfeeding is safer, easier, faster, more economical and more convenient. There's no formula to buy, mix, refrigerate and reheat, and no bottles and nipples to sterilize.
- Breast milk is more easily digestible. Breastfed babies have fewer feeding problems and intestinal disorders.
- Breastfed babies have fewer skin disorders and allergies.
- Breastfeeding is reported to have the potential to prevent obesity in children.
- Breast milk is sterile and always fresh.

- Recent studies indicate breast-fed infants may be less likely to fall victim to sudden infant death syndrome (SIDS) than those fed cow's milk or formula.

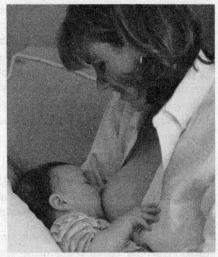

Nursing can also provide benefits to the mother. Most nursing mothers find it a satisfying and enjoyable experience. Breastfeeding develops a close mother-baby attachment that extends far beyond infancy.

Besides the close psychological bond established between mother and child, nursing supplies a physical phenomenon. Breastfeeding aids in restoring your figure more quickly to its normal, non-pregnant state. As the baby sucks on the nipple, contractions of the uterus are stimulated which help to expel any remaining bits of tissue lining the uterus. These contractions during nursing also help "firm" the uterus, which helps control bleeding.

If a nursing mother does need to be away for a feeding or two, her baby can be given a bottle feeding. By planning ahead, a mother can express milk by hand or with the aid of a breast pump, to store for later use.

Should it be necessary to store your breast milk, remember that it can lose its nutritive value as well as spoil if not properly stored. In an article appearing in the January 2001 issue of the *American Academy of Pediatricians News,* pediatricians were encouraged to assure parents that refrigeration of breast milk for up to 72 hours was safe. Breast milk will keep for several weeks in a freezer if temperature is maintained below 30° F. In a deep freezer at 0° F, the milk should be able to stay for several months. Fresh breast milk should be used as much as possible, with frozen breast milk used only as a back-up.

Breast milk, when removed from the refrigerator or freezer, may appear discolored (yellow tinged, bluish green, even a little brown). This does not mean the breast milk is bad. Always check breast milk to be certain it does not smell sour or taste bad. Because breast milk does not look like cow's milk when stored, taste and smell, not color, should determine if the refrigerated breast milk is good.

Breast milk thaws quite rapidly. The best way to accomplish this is by placing the container of frozen milk in a bowl under running lukewarm water. After it is thawed, shake the bottle or container to ensure even temperature.

Never heat breast milk in a microwave oven. The high temperature can destroy some of the vitamins and protective cells. Because the milk heats unevenly, the outside container can feel cool, but the milk may be very hot and cause a burn.

Before feeding, always test a few drops on your wrist to be certain milk is near body temperature.

A nursing mother should eat the same well-balanced diet as any other adult. It is advisable to increase liquids—water, milk and juices— and add about 500 calories of nutritious food per day. These extra calories are easily burned up while you are nursing, so you won't need to worry about them affecting your weight. Remember, if you do feel the need to lose weight, avoid dieting until after you've stopped nursing. You need adequate calories and good nutrition while you are breastfeeding.

Formula feeding

Doctors enthusiastically advocate breastfeeding and encourage their patients to consider it and at least give it a fair trial. Formula feeding is an option that has been successful with millions of babies who have grown and developed normally. Bottle feeding has both advantages and disadvantages. With bottle feeding, you can more easily determine whether the

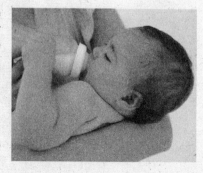

child is sufficiently satisfied because you have control over and knowledge of the amount of formula your baby drinks. For example, you can easily increase the amount of formula per feeding if you find that your baby still seems hungry after an initial feeding. Bottle fed babies tend to require fewer feedings fairly soon, although you still need to plan time each day for preparing the formula. Bottle feeding enables your partner or someone else to take over some of the night feedings. And when feeding from a bottle, your baby will still be held in your arms and feel your love and affection from the experience.

One disadvantage is that colic and other intestinal disorders are not uncommon among babies fed from a bottle. This may be cause for some anxiety and frustration until the best and most satisfactory formula is determined for your baby.

Certainly it is true that the advantages of breastfeeding far outweigh those of bottle feeding, but with either option, think over the various advantages and disadvantages discussed here. Your final decision should not be based on the advice of friends. If you are a healthy mother, and most are, you should

Three ways to burp your baby
Whether you are nursing or bottle feeding, you can make your baby more comfortable after eating by gently burping him or her. If you don't know how to "burp" the baby, the nurse or an experienced mother will show you what to do. Pick him up and hold him against you. Gently pat him in the middle of his back. Don't pound or slap him. If he doesn't burp, a change of position may help. Put him down on his stomach for a moment. Then lift him to your shoulder again. If baby still doesn't burp, leave him alone. Sometimes the baby doesn't need to burp and you shouldn't exhaust yourself or the baby by trying to force him.

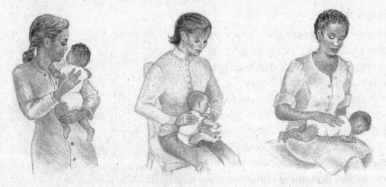

try breastfeeding and then decide whether you want to continue with it. If, for some reason, you cannot breastfeed, you should not feel guilty. Your baby can still grow up healthy and well adjusted if he or she is fed from a bottle.

You really don't have to make your final decision until after the baby is born. Then decide with your clinician whether you will breast or bottle feed your baby.

Telling other children about the baby

If you have older children, when is the best time to tell them about the new brother or sister who will be joining the family? It really depends upon the ages of the older children. But regardless of age, it is always best to inform them before going to the hospital and the baby is born. An older child should not be suddenly surprised with a newborn baby as though the baby were a new toy. Let your common sense and intelligence guide you when deciding the appropriate time to convey the news. Here are some suggestions that may help you with possible approaches to the issue.

Because your 2-, 3-, or 4-year-old children have little concept of time, it is unnecessary to tell them from the moment you are pregnant. Children have difficulty distinguishing between tomorrow and 8 months from now, so there is no need to burden them with the suspense. A good time to tell them is about the 4th or 5th month, when your abdomen is obviously growing larg-er. By then your child will probably recognize that something important is about to happen. Since the lives of the other children will certainly be affect-ed, they will want to know what is going on and should be told.

A natural and intelligent method of breaking the news is for the mother to casually and simply take the child aside and say, "Soon there will be a new baby in the house." You could then explain what babies look like and what will happen to the family when the baby arrives. Some questions should be avoided. For example, do not ask your child: "How would you like to share your room?" or "How would you like to sleep in a big bed so that the new baby can have your crib?" Both questions are likely to elicit a negative response from the child.

Your attitude needs to be positive and firm as you plan for the new addition to your household. Try to help the older children of school age see the arrival of the baby as an event that is exciting and one in which they will continue

to be important and necessary. For example, you could take them to a maternity hospital or show them pictures in a book to help eliminate their apprehensions. Include them when you begin planning the baby's room. One good way to make older children feel involved is to give them additional small responsibilities as though they are helping you. Depending on their ages and capabilities, small chores like making beds or cleaning tables can give them the sense that they are being helpful. They will then enjoy their new importance and independence and understand the reasons behind it.

There are also some attitudes you should avoid. Do not give the older child the impression that the new baby is taking his or her place, and do not tell older children that the attention which they formerly received must now be shared. In fact, it is important to give the older children even more attention when you bring the new baby home. Another good idea is to keep a few items on hand to give to the other children when friends send gifts to the baby. Whenever you think that the older children need it, you should bestow your attention on them because young children need constant reassurance that they are loved. Occasionally you may even want to express some slight annoyance toward the new baby so that the older children will be reassured that the baby is not the center of the universe. Keeping your other children feeling important, loved, and involved can be a delicate balancing act, but it will pay dividends in avoiding unnecessary problems later.

Information on complex topics like jealousy and rivalry can be found in other books that your pediatrician can recommend. Books can be helpful as guidelines, but do not substitute them for your own thinking when problems arise. The best decisions you make concerning the raising of your children will come from your intelligence, your practical experience, and your common sense.

Preparations for your return home

During the latter part of your pregnancy, you should make plans to have someone at home to help you when you return from the hospital. At delivery time it would be wise to have a familiar person in your home to care for the other children. This can be a family member or friend. Perhaps a few friends can alternate, each helping out a day at a time.

Your brief stay in the hospital after hours of labor and delivery may leave you exhausted. Do not expect to return home from the hospital with your baby and immediately step back in to your previous household routine along with caring for your new baby. Try to arrange for a mother's helper or housekeeper to be at your home when you arrive from the hospital. It will be worth the cost.

Fatigue is to be expected during those first few weeks postpartum. Arrange to take naps while your baby is sleeping. Let someone else clean the house or prepare a meal. You can often find a nurse or helper through your hospital, clinician, or a friend's recommendation. Arrange for someone to begin a week after your due date. The additional rest you get during those first weeks home will allow you to regain your strength and emotional well-being more rapidly.

Your partner, and older children if you have any, should also assume a few more chores until you get your strength back.

Your baby's doctor

Planning ahead should not only include your needs, it is also the time to select a doctor for your baby. Your baby's doctor could be your family physician or a pediatrician. He or she should check your baby before you are discharged from the hospital. If the doctor you have selected is not on staff at the hospital where your baby is, ask your clinician to arrange for a hospital resident or staff member to examine your baby before you bring him/her home.

During your baby's first year, he or she will need to be checked once a month, unless there is a problem requiring more frequent visits. As a rule, visits to the baby's doctor during his or her second year of life are once every three months. At these visits, the baby's weight and development will be checked. If necessary, changes may be made in the feeding schedule, and required inoculations will be administered. Should any problems arise such as colic, rashes or digestive disorders, the doctor you selected will be familiar with your baby and better able to make recommendations.

Packing a bag for the hospital

If your hospital requires a reservation, you or your healthcare provider can make one at the appropriate time prior to your due date. The hospital will take care of many of your needs, so there won't be a great many items you'll need to bring. For example, nightgowns and basic sanitary items are provided.

For style and comfort, you can certainly improve on some of what is provided in the hospital. Which is why it is a good idea to have an overnight bag packed and ready in case you have to leave for the hospital in a hurry. The following is a list of basic items you will need, but if you happen to forget a few, do not worry. The hospital gift shop stocks some items, or your partner can bring any others when coming to visit you.

Bring with you:

- Bathrobe, flat slippers
- Two or three nightgowns (perhaps with a front opening for breast feeding)
- Toothbrush and toothpaste, deodorant
- Hairbrush, comb, compact, and other cosmetics
- One or two bras the same size as you wore when pregnant, or nursing bras if you plan to nurse
- A book or some magazines
- Small change
- Loose fitting clothes to wear home
- Camera with film and batteries
- Insurance card and identification

What to have ready for baby

While the baby is in the nursery, the hospital will provide diapers and shirts, but when you take your baby home, you will need the following items:

- Two or three diapers
- Waterproof panties
- Cotton shirt
- Diaper safety pins if using cloth diapers
- Wrapper
- Knit Cap
- Blankets or bunting

Depending on the weather, the nurse will advise you on what you need and will help you dress the baby for going home. Also, before bringing the baby home, remember to install the infant car carrier (see pages 125-126).

Planning for the homecoming

The baby's furniture and nursery items
It is a good idea to get things ready before the baby is born because you will have more time to make careful selections. On a practical level, a sturdy, well-made, full-size crib is your best investment because your baby can use it until the age of 2 or 3. You might think this crib looks gigantic, but remember that time passes quickly. Money spent on fancy furniture is really fulfilling your desires, not the baby's. For example, there are beautifully decorated bassinets available, but they are not practical because the baby outgrows them in a month or two. You can also buy a small-size crib, but again, the baby will outgrow it by the 4th month.

The American Academy of Pediatrics has issued the following crib safety recommendations:

- Crib slats must not be more than 2 3/8 inches apart to prevent the baby from catching his or her head between the slats.
- When lowered, the crib sides should be 4 inches above the top of the mattress or 9 inches above the mattress support.
- When the mattress is placed in its lowest position and the crib side is up, there should be 22 to 26 inches from the top of the side rail to the mattress support.

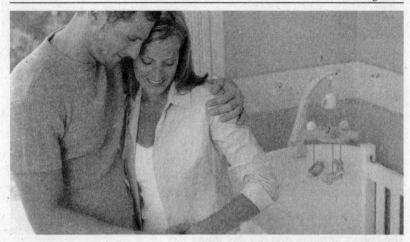

- The sides must be operated with a locking latch that cannot be accidentally released.

- The mattress must be the same size as the crib so that it fits snugly into the crib frame. This is to prevent the baby from wedging his/her body between the mattress and crib side, and suffocating. For the same reason, a bumper guard should be used until the child is able to stand on their own. The mattress cover should be moisture-proof and easy to clean.

- The surfaces of the crib should be free of splinters and cracks, and painted with non-toxic, lead-free paint. The latches and hardware should not have rough edges.

It is a good idea to buy sturdy furniture that is well made because it will get a great deal of wear and tear. You can purchase a dresser that matches the crib, and there are furniture sets available which can grow with your baby. In other words, as time passes, you can add a toy chest, desk or other dressers, all of which match the crib.

What else will you need? A night light is essential. Many mothers recommend a dressing or changing table with drawers for diapers and clothing. This eliminates the strain caused by bending over to change and bathe the baby. Washable throw rugs are preferable to wall-to-wall carpeting because the latter retains too much dust. Be sure to have a non-slip pad under the rug to prevent slipping or falling while carrying the baby. Eventually you will need a high chair and a stroller.

Car carriers

You must have a car carrier for the baby. The recommended car safety seat is a high-backed, molded bucket seat which faces the rear of the car, never the front.

Several infant-only seat models come with detachable bases. The base attaches to the car and the car seat snaps into the base. The base must fit tightly into the car. In some cases the seat may fit better without the base. Infant seats come with a 3-point harness or a 5-point harness. The disadvantage is that an infant seat must be replaced by a convertible one when baby reaches about 20 pounds.

The advantage of the convertible car seat is that it fits a child from 7 to 8 pounds to about 40 pounds. The disadvantage is that it is bulky and less portable than an infant car seat.

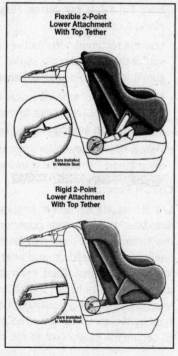

According to an article in the August 2002 issue of the *American Academy of Pediatrics News,* about 80 percent of car seats are installed incorrectly. To locate a free seat-inspection-facility, contact **866-732-8243** or **www.seatcheck.org.**

Important points to remember:

- Federal regulations state no child 12 years of age or younger should ride in the front seat of a car with a passenger side air bag.

- The rear seat is generally the safest position for any child.

- Always put your baby in the back seat of your car, facing the rear.

- Use a rear-facing car seat for babies weighing up to 20 pounds and as close to 1-year-old as possible. There are some infant carriers for use up to 35 pounds.

- Car seats come with a 3-point harness or a 5-point harness. The harness holds the baby in the car seat. The vehicle's seat belt holds the seat in the car. Both the seat belt and harness must be snugly attached to prevent injury.

- Secure the baby in the car carrier every time you take the baby in the car, even for a 2-minute trip to the corner drugstore.

- Be certain that an inherited, borrowed or used carrier meets the current recommended safety requirements. If you are unsure about how a previously owned carrier should be used, contact the manufacturer for an instruction manual.

- Do not substitute a household infant seat used for feeding or carrying the baby for a safe car carrier. Regular infant seats are not designed to withstand a collision.

- Use the recommended carrier until the child outgrows the toddler model. If you obtain a convertible carrier, which can go from infant to toddler use, be sure that you top-anchor the seat according to its instructions for toddler use.

- Universal use of safe infant car carriers would eliminate most of the almost 70,000 injuries each year to babies and toddlers in automobile accidents, injuries which are the leading cause of death among young children.

- Follow the manufacturer's instructions on how to use your car seat; always keep these instructions with the car seat.

LATCH Program

LATCH stands for Lower Anchors and Tethers for Children. It is a system mandated by the federal government in an effort to standardize and simplify the installation of child restraints. Nearly all new vehicles and child safety seats manufactured on and after September 1, 2002 will be equipped with the LATCH system. Cars, minivans and light trucks will be required to have anchor points between the vehicle's seat cushion and the seat back in at least 2 rear seating positions. Child safety seats will have tether straps or rigid connectors that hook into these anchors, thereby eliminating the need to secure the safety seat to the vehicle using the vehicle's seat belt system.

Transporting premature and low birth-weight infants

The following guidelines were issued by the American Academy of Pediatrics for transporting premature and low birth-weight infants:

- Look for either an infant-only car seat with a 3-part harness system or a convertible car seat with a 5-part harness system.

- Do not place a small baby in a car safety seat with a shield, abdominal pad or arm rest that could come in contact with the baby's face and neck during impact.

- Baby should be positioned with buttocks and back flat against the back of the car seat. Rolled-up blankets may be placed on both sides of the infant to help support his/her head and neck. A rolled-up diaper or small blanket can be inserted between the crotch strap and the baby, so that baby will not slouch forward in the car safety seat.

- Premature infants born less than 37 weeks gestation should be observed in a car safety seat before being discharged from the hospital, so that the baby can be monitored for possible breathing problems, drop in heart rate, or changes in blood oxygen levels. Check with your hospital to see if it has developed policies to include this procedure in their discharge planning process.

- Babies with documented evidence of a decrease in blood oxygen levels, lapses in breathing, or a drop in the heart rate when placed upright in a car seat should not travel in conventional car safety seats. They should be transported in special safety devices that allow babies to be on their backs or tummies while in transport. Infant swings, seats and carriers should also be avoided for these infants.

- If heart and breathing monitors are prescribed for the baby, parents should use the equipment while traveling, using a portable, self-contained power source.

Baby's Clothes

Shopping for the baby can be fun, but it is also easy to overdo it. Remember that your baby will outgrow small clothes quickly, so you do not really need to buy more than is necessary. The time of the year when your baby will be born should be considered. The following list is a good foundation, and as you get to know your baby, you can add those items that work best for you.

- 2 to 4 dozen diapers (1 dozen is enough if you plan to use diaper services or disposable diapers)
- A package of diaper pins if using cloth diapers
- 6 undershirts (sleeve length depends on the weather)
- 6 nightgowns or 1-piece pajamas
- 6 pairs waterproof pants if using cloth diapers
- 2 sweaters, 1 wool or synthetic and 1 cotton
- 4 flannel receiving blankets
- 3 contour sheets for crib, and flannel-covered rubber sheeting to place beneath the sheet to protect the mattress
- Quilted mattress pad—to be placed between sheet and rubber sheeting so the baby won't perspire excessively
- A baby bunting or snow suit for cool weather
- Woolen blanket
- A washable cotton blanket

Diapers are available in different types with varying amounts of absorbency and softness. Some are sewn with extra layers of absorbency in the center where it is needed. Other types are pre-shaped. Disposable diapers are also an option if your budget can afford the expense. You should be careful that they do not cause irritation or diaper rash on your baby. Look over the whole range of products before you make a selection. Trial and error in selecting your baby's clothes will ultimately result in what works best for you.

Baby's bath needs

You will need the following items for the baby's bath:

- Changing table—optional but convenient for changing, bathing and dressing the baby.
- Plastic infant bathtub that fits over the sink or on countertop for bathing. A large plastic dishpan may be used instead, or you can line your kitchen sink with a large towel and bathe the baby there if it is warm enough
- Large plastic diaper pail with lid.

- 2 to 4 soft towels and 3 soft washcloths (you don't need to buy new ones, use clean soft bath towels you already have on-hand).

- 2 large, soft towels, 1 to cover the changing table.

- Mild soap.

- Sterile cotton.

- Cotton-tipped applicators.

- Baby shampoo.

- Rectal thermometer.

Feeding supplies

If you will be bottle feeding your child, the following items are recommended:

- 8 bottles with nipples and caps, 8-ounce size. These are available in boilable plastic as well as glass. You may also want to buy a few 4-ounce bottles for water, but the 8-ounce bottles are sufficient.

- A 32-ounce measuring pitcher.

- Funnel.

- Tongs for taking bottles out of boiling water.

- Extra nipples.

- Bottle sterilizer or large pot.

- If you breastfeed, you will want a few bottles for water, supplemental feedings, or expressed-milk feedings.

It is a good idea to investigate the selection of disposable bottles available and discuss them with your clinician. All of these items can be purchased at the drugstore.

Before you take your baby home your clinician will advise you about the formula preparation.

Repairing used equipment

If you buy or inherit used equipment, the Consumer Product Safety Commission recommends that you check and repair latches and harnesses and scrape or sand off all old paint. Refinish with lead-free, household enamel paint (check the label).

Chapter 12 Going to the hospital

*D*ELIVERING A BABY IS OFTEN THE FIRST hospital experience for many women. Even if you have been treated previously in a hospital, you'll see that the maternity process is different from any other. Most times, no one is really sick on a maternity floor. Women arriving there are looking forward to a positive experience. Consequently, the maternity sections of hospitals tend to be cheerful, friendly places.

Let's look step-by-step at the process of an expectant mother's delivery in the hospital, beginning with her time at home just prior to leaving. Knowing what to expect will reduce your anxiety and help you feel more relaxed.

Notify your healthcare provider at the first sign of labor. He or she can discuss the timing of your contractions and instruct you when to leave for the hospital. By now, you or your partner should have already arranged for the care of your other children. Your partner should be dressed and ready to leave with you. Don't forget your pre-packed suitcase, and remember, don't rush.

Admissions

You will arrive at the hospital where your clinician is a staff member. Registration at the hospital can be accomplished in one of 3 ways:

1. You can pre-register before arrival, in which case some hospitals may take you directly to your room.

2. Someone may register for you upon arrival.

3. You will register at the admitting office when you arrive. The admitting secretary will ask you for some necessary information, including your name, address, phone number, next of kin, etc.

It is also important for you to have the card and number of your hospital insurance plan available, if you have one, as well as any personal identification the hospital may require.

Though it may seem longer, this only takes a few minutes. As the secretary proceeds to gather information, your contractions will continue. When the secretary is finished, a nurse will arrive, place you in a wheelchair, and take you and your partner to the maternity unit.

Preparation

Depending on the facility, your partner will probably be allowed to accompany you, but may initially be directed to a special waiting area. A nurse will help you undress and you will be given a hospital gown. Your clothes will be tagged and placed with your suitcase. Although hospitals are conscientious about identifying your belongings, it is wise to leave jewelry and any other valuables at home.

The hospital staff will then help you into bed and begin the steps in your preparation for delivering your baby. Hospitals follow different procedures, so ask your clinician or childbirth educator about the preparation process at your hospital so there will be no surprises. The "prep" will include an assessment of your blood pressure, pulse, respirations, fetal heartbeat and contractions. The nurse or other health care provider may do a vaginal examination to check cervical changes. Rarely, a cleansing or shaving of the pubic area, or an enema may be ordered. Each step of the preparation has a purpose. The information that you have given will be recorded for the clinician to study when he or she sees you. You should also not be surprised if your doctor does not appear immediately.

Single room maternity care

More and more hospitals, and all birthing centers, now have single-room maternity care centers. Everything takes place here— the labor, delivery, recovery and postpartum period— so that you spend your entire stay in the hospital in the same room. This room has several chairs or couches as well as a bed for family members or support persons who are with you. There is also a private bath with a shower and/or a bathtub. The necessary equipment for the birth and care of the baby will be located either in this room or in an accessible location nearby.

Other hospitals may have the labor, delivery and recovery rooms (LDR) combined but transfer you after delivery to a postpartum unit where you continue to rest until you go home.

Traditional labor and delivery suites

Other hospitals continue to have traditional labor and delivery suites where you are evaluated for labor in one room, transferred to a labor room for the duration of the labor, to the delivery room for the birth, then to a recovery room to recover prior to being transferred to the post-partum unit. The delivery room is similar to an operating room. You would move to a delivery table and your legs would be lifted into supports. Ask your clinician which type of facility is available where you will be giving birth.

Unless an emergency arises, the baby's father should be able to remain with you for the birth.

Birthing room

An alternative to the "labor-delivery-recovery rooms" procedure that is now being offered by many hospitals is the birthing room. This alternative has been designed for couples who want a family-oriented experience, or who might have wanted to deliver their child at home but were concerned about medical safety. Designed to resemble a home-like sitting room and bedroom, the birthing room in a hospital offers an atmosphere of privacy in order to provide a family-centered birth experience. In the atmosphere of surroundings that are similar to home, the mother labors, delivers and recovers. Accompanying the mother in the birthing room are the partner, perhaps other family members and friends, and depending on the hospital, even older children. Because the birthing room is inside a hospital, the mother can be easily moved into the conventional facilities if problems develop during any stage of labor or delivery. The home-like birthing room allows for a "bonding period" in which the new parents have immediate physical contact and can cuddle their new baby. In addition, the mother can even begin breastfeeding within 10 or 15 minutes of birth. Along with rooming-in later, the experience of the birthing room is intended to help the family establish their new relationships before they return home.

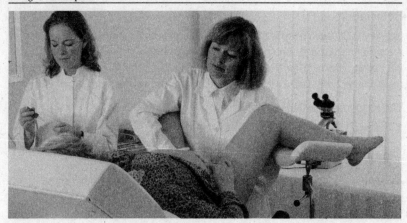

These facilities are not available for high-risk expectant mothers. The health and safety of mother and child remain the most important priorities of childbirth. Consequently, high-risk mothers and babies may be required to have a more conventional delivery to take advantage of sophisticated equipment and techniques.

The hospital nursery

You and your partner will have time to become acquainted with your newborn either in the delivery room or the birthing room. Following this, your baby will be identified, weighed, measured, bathed and examined. A complete physical examination of the baby will follow within a few hours, with all the findings reported to you.

Your baby will remain in the hospital nursery, except for feedings, unless you have a rooming-in or LDRP plan. The nursery provides an unobstructed view of the babies being diapered, dressed and fed. Most of the time, they will be sleeping. Sometimes, particularly before feeding times, they may be crying. Nurses are in constant attendance, closely observing all babies. You will be constantly encouraged to visit and hold your baby, or the nurses will bring the baby to your room.

Rooming-in

Nursery facilities in hospitals take care of the needs of many newborn babies as we described above. Another alternative available at many hospitals is a service called "rooming-in." Rather than keeping the baby in a large nursery, the mother keeps her baby with her in the same room or in a small area nearby.

The rooming-in arrangement has primarily 3 benefits.

1. As soon as the mother has rested sufficiently, she can tend to her baby herself. Depending on the hospital, there are several modifications to this plan.

2. Rooming-in permits immediate parent-child contact called bonding, which parents and babies thrive on.

3. If a woman is having her first child, rooming-in is helpful because she can learn to care for her baby under the hospital's supervision.

There is one drawback, however. New mothers need all the rest they can get. A conventional hospital nursery provides more rest time for the mother than does rooming-in. If your hospital has a rooming-in plan, weigh the benefits of having your baby with you as opposed to being in the nursery.

Bonding

Two Cleveland physicians have defined bonding as "a unique relationship between two persons that endures through time." Early bonding consists of close physical and emotional attachment. Cuddling, kissing, holding and breastfeeding are important in bonding. Eye contact is also important, and it has been shown that a baby can often follow the parent's eyes immediately after birth.

The topic of bonding has been widely discussed, and researchers have noted that early parent-child bonding (from birth to 3 years) is important in the development of the child and in the development of parent-child relationships. Some of the evidence available also suggests that bonding strengthens the family group and causes a decrease in child abuse.

Bonding is most easily accomplished in the birthing room or rooming-in facilities, but if you cannot take advantage of these options, you can still establish close contact with your baby in the delivery room, during feeding and later at home.

What a healthy newborn baby looks like

Many mothers honestly admitted that they were surprised by the appearance of their babies after birth. It is not unusual for a newborn to appear swollen and with puffy eyes. Compared to an older child, a newborn's head is often elongated and out of proportion to the rest of the body.

Most of the photographs you see which are supposedly of newborns are really pictures of infants 1 or 2 months old. Be assured your baby's appearance will be different 1 month and even 1 week after delivery. A picture and description of a 1-week-old baby appears on page 178.

Chapter 13 Becoming a mother

*N*OW THAT THE STAGE IS SET FOR GIVING BIRTH and becoming a mother, you may have a number of questions about what will happen during labor and delivery. How will I really know when I am in labor? What if I am out when it happens? Will I reach the hospital in time? What if my clinician is not home when I need him/her?

You may also have heard stories about ambulances with screeching sirens roaring through the streets or mothers giving birth in the back seat of a taxi cab. But the truth is that most deliveries are normal, uneventful and proceed in a routine fashion. The reason you hear about dramatic deliveries in the news media is that those deliveries are so rare.

How to tell when labor begins

As indicated earlier, your delivery will probably occur somewhere between 2 weeks before and 2 weeks after your due date. Only a few women deliver on, or within a day or two of their due date. Your natural apprehension and impatience during this time can be eased if you understand the process of labor and recognize what is happening to you. As your baby prepares to emerge into the outside world, it will change its position and your uterus will sink forward and downward. When these changes occur, observant, experienced friends may say to you, "Your baby has dropped. It looks like you're ready to go."

Some other changes may take place as well. There may be an increase in vaginal discharge. As the baby shifts position, you may notice that former backaches and abdominal pressure have now become leg pains. This is because different muscles are now supporting the load. You might also notice that your clothes fit differently.

All of these changes indicate that the baby is assuming its birth position, and its head will be pushing against the cervix, as shown on page 141. "Lightening" is the term used to describe this new positioning, and there may be some intermittent pain and discomfort at this time. If you are having your first baby and do not know what real contractions feel like, you may mistakenly think that this "lightening" is the start of labor. Very often such mothers call their clinician or even go to the hospital, but then nothing else happens. During these false alarms, the contractions are far apart and irregular. After checking you over, you will be sent home to wait for the beginning of real labor. It is frustrating for a woman to continue to wait patiently, but clinicians know that such "false alarms" occur frequently.

Remember that real labor can occur on the night of a "false alarm" or a week or two later. The actual date when your baby will be born varies from woman to woman, and no one can determine the exact time.

How will you know when real labor begins? There are 3 main signs that you will recognize:

1. Contractions will occur with timed regularity. At the beginning, your contractions may last 45 seconds to a minute, and occur every 10, 15 or 20 minutes. An hour or two later, they will be more frequent. A contraction begins lightly across the back and then slowly builds in intensity like a wave as it travels across the abdomen. The reason for these contractions is that the muscles of the uterus are preparing to push the baby from the uterus.

   Many doctors ask their patients to notify them when contractions are five to eight minutes apart. This will vary based on your particular situation and the preference of your clinician. That's why it's important that you ask your clinician when you should call.

   To help distinguish between true labor and false labor pains see the chart on page 139.

2. Bright red bleeding must be reported immediately. However, blood tinged mucus called "show" may occur before real labor, sometime even several days or weeks before labor begins. During pregnancy this mucus acts like a plug sealing the neck of the uterus. Sometimes when labor is about to start the mucus is dislodged and travels down through the vagina. If you are concerned about the amount or type of bleeding, please contact your clinician.

3. Your membranes rupture. There may be a gush of watery liquid or a slow leak from the vagina. You may have heard this referred to as "your bag of water breaking."

   This liquid is called amniotic fluid, and its job was to cushion the baby. The liquid is discharged as the uterus contracts and the birth passage opens. The membranes usually rupture toward the end of labor, but sometimes it can rupture earlier. You should contact your clinician if they rupture, even if you are away from home. The gush of water means that your real labor may be starting, and you should be ready to go to the hospital. Be ready to decribe the color and consistency of the fluid. If you are unable to reach your clinician, go directly to the hospital.

There is an additional sign your clinician will look for called effacement. Effacement is the thinning out and softening of the cervix. In most cases, labor will not progress until the cervical canal softens and begins to thin even if the membranes have ruptured. This softening and thinning of the cervix is also known as cervical ripening.

A final word of advice: when real labor begins, refrain from eating or drinking—ice chips, however, are permissible. Should you need an anesthetic, a full stomach could cause nausea and vomiting, and result in aspirating food or fluid into the lungs.

When to call your clinician

The 3 signs of real labor may occur all at the same time, or they may occur in any order at different times. Knowing this, when should you call your clinician? If your membranes rupture, you should call whether you experience any discomfort or not. If "show" (the mucus-like, bloody discharge that is one sign of labor) appears, you know that real labor may soon be starting.

Contractions		
	True labor	**False labor**
Frequency of	Regular with contractions getting closer and closer	Irregular
Intensity of	Progressively more painful	No increase — not that painful
Length of	40 to 60 seconds	Irregular
Site of	Upper abdomen or lower back — radiates to lower abdomen	Lower abdomen

By itself, "show" does not warrant calling the clinician, though you may want to alert him or her. It is also important to understand that first-time babies take their time being born. The reason is that the birth passage is tense and unyielding because it has not been used before. Many healthcare providers request they be notified when contractions are 5 to 8 minutes apart. This may vary, so be sure to ask your clinician when he or she wants to be called. If you live a distance away, you will have to factor in the amount of time it takes to get to the hospital. Remember, it is better to arrive at the hospital a bit early. A previous delivery often affects (shortens) the timing of the next delivery.

Despite what you might hear, most babies are not born at night. Those births just seem more vivid and memorable. Regardless of the time, notify your clinician when your membranes rupture or when Stage 1 of labor begins.

What happens during labor?

The entire labor process lasts an average of 12 to 14 hours for a first birth. Generally, subsequent labors are shorter. Most of your work will occur during the first and second stages. Learning muscle relaxation and breathing techniques better prepares you for these stages of labor. It is important to try and relax, even read a magazine during contractions if possible. As a woman, your body is designed and prepared for childbirth. Your clinician and the hospital staff are there to keep you safe and comfortable at this special time.

First stage: The first stage of labor, what is referred to as the cervical dilation stage, begins with the onset of real labor until the cervix is fully dilated. Regular contractions are a sign of labor. In most cases, the baby's head is down, pressing against the cervix (see Fig. 1). As the cervix dilates further, contractions get closer together. Try not to bear down or push with each contraction at this time. The first stage is usually the longest of the 3 stages, and ends when the cervix is fully dilated (10 cm). Contractions come every 2-3 minutes and may last as long as 60 seconds.

Second stage: The baby is born during the second stage. Beginning when the cervix is fully dilated, it may last anywhere from 5 minutes to over 2 hours. The second stage ends with the birth of the baby. It is at this stage that your clinician will ask you to push with each contraction.

The unique physiological changes that occur in a woman during pregnancy prepare the vagina for its elastic function. While it is normally a thin tube-shaped organ, it is now greatly distended. The baby descends further down the cervical canal and into the vagina with each contraction and bearing-down motion. The initial view of the top of baby's head as it moves down the birth canal is called crowning.

First the head emerges, then shoulders, trunk, and finally feet. As the baby emerges, the clinician grasps the head and helps guide the baby through. If the umbilical cord is wrapped around the baby's neck, it is removed from this position before delivering the rest of the baby.

Any mucus or other amniotic residue is quickly suctioned from the baby's mouth and nose as the head emerges. The baby begins to breathe regularly and utters his or her first cry. Following the baby's delivery, mother and baby are still attached by the umbilical cord. The cord is clamped and then cut.

The baby will be quickly dried and wrapped in blankets, placed into a heated bassinet or on your belly for warmth. Drops or ointment will be put into the baby's eyes to prevent infection. Almost every jurisdiction requires by law that newborns be given this eye medication. Identification bands are placed on mother and baby before leaving the delivery room. Hand and foot prints may also be taken of the baby.

Newborn babies have very small amounts of vitamin K, which promotes normal blood clotting. For this reason, the baby may be given a shot of vitamin K. In about a week, the baby will produce sufficient quantities of vitamin K on his/her own. Standard procedures vary in hospitals, but soon after stage 2, the parents are allowed to hold the baby and can begin to establish a bond with him/her.

Third stage: Now that the baby has arrived, the mother still has one last stage in the delivery that must be completed. This stage is also called the "placental" stage because it involves delivery of the afterbirth, or placenta, the structure through which the fetus derives nourishment in order to develop. Usually it takes only a few minutes to extract the placenta and other membranes.

Figure 1. As labor progresses, the cervix becomes thinner and more dilated.

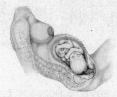

Figure 2. The membranes forming the bag of water rupture.

Figure 3. The head molds to the shape of the pelvis as the baby gradually descends in the birth canal.

Figure 4. Baby slowly rotates as descent continues.

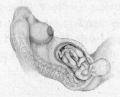

Figure 5. Baby's head emerges.

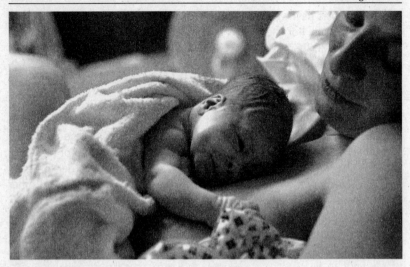

Apgar

As a part of her interest in a baby's response to birth and life on his or her own, Dr. Virginia Apgar developed a score to assess several key indicators of the baby's well-being. Practically all babies are assigned an Apgar score, taken at 1 minute after birth and again at 5 minutes as part of the monitoring process. The five characteristics are assigned a number from 0 to 2, and the Apgar score is the total of those numbers. Although the Apgar score is a good tool that assists in understanding the baby's progress at a given time, it does not by itself show how well the baby did before birth or what the future will hold. Other signs will also be checked to provide more complete information on the baby's general health.

A = appearance or color

P = pulse (heart rate)

G = grimace or reflex irritability

A = activity

R = respiration

For each sign, a score of 2 is given if the sign in the baby is normal. If a sign is missing, then a score of 0 is assigned. A score of 1 is given if the sign is present but below normal. As a general rule, a score of 7 or more (after 5 minutes) is considered normal. However, many doctors do not place as much significance on the Apgar score today as they once did. If the newborn shows breathing or circulation problems, doctors do not wait a full minute to take action. Also, many babies who may have lower scores at birth ultimately turn out to be healthy.

Episiotomy

An episiotomy is a small incision (cut) the clinician makes in the vagina and the perineum at the time of delivery. Though the vagina possesses great elasticity, there are times when the vaginal tissue is stretched so thinly that to keep the tissue from tearing, an episiotomy is performed. An episiotomy also helps relieve pressure on the baby's head. Not all women need an episiotomy. After delivery the incision is stitched closed. In the past, episiotomy was routinely performed. Current evidence recommends against this practice and advises clinicians to only perform after they have weighed the risks and benefits. If you have any questions regarding episiotomy, it is wise to discuss this issue during your regular prenatal visits.

Analgesics and Anesthetics

There are 2 categories of drugs/medications clinicians administer prior to or during delivery of a baby. The first, known as analgesics, are drugs which help relieve pain without causing a loss of consciousness. Analgesics help relax you between contractions.

Common Analgesics

1. Clinicians sometimes use narcotic drugs to reduce pain and enhance relaxation, and there may be a need to repeat the doses. A good example of such a common narcotic drug is Demerol. There are 3 possible disadvantages with the use of narcotic drugs:

    — if given too early, the drug may slow down labor

    — if given too late, the drug may not provide adequate pain relief

    — some women may experience nausea and sleepiness.

2. Tranquilizers will relieve anxiety and alleviate nausea and vomiting. They also enhance the effect of, and thus reduce the amount of, narcotics that are needed. Examples of tranquilizers are: Atarax, Phenergan, Sparine, Thorazine, Visatril, and Valium. The possible disadvantages are that they may cause dizziness, drowsiness, dry mouth, or blurred vision.

3. The effect of barbiturates can be hypnotic and sleep-inducing. They are often given in combination with narcotics to relieve apprehension very early in labor, but they have little effect on pain. Amytal and Seconal are examples of barbiturates. One possible disadvantage is that they must not be given too close to delivery because they can cause a sleepy baby.

Analgesic drugs are given in small doses and are usually avoided shortly before delivery to avoid such side effects as drowsiness or decreased ability of the mother to concentrate. Clinicians must monitor all of these common medications carefully because they can cross the placenta slowing the baby's reflexes and breathing at birth.

The other category of drugs is called anesthetics. An anesthetic causes complete loss of feeling or sensation. An anesthetic can be general or regional. A general anesthetic causes a state of complete unconsciousness with a total absence of pain or sensation over the entire body. General anesthetics are occasionally used for cesarean deliveries or, on rare occasion, for emergency vaginal delivery. It is not given to relieve labor pains. It is essential that no food be eaten prior to a general anesthetic to avoid food or acid from the stomach being aspirated into the lungs or windpipe.

A regional (local) anesthetic produces a total lack of pain in a given area by interrupting the sensory nerve pathway from the region of the body where it is injected. There is no loss of consciousness with a regional anesthetic.

Common regional anesthetics

1. *Epidural block:* This anesthetic affects a larger area, causing a loss of sensation in the lower half of the body. The mother is awake during labor and delivery. The local anesthetic is injected into a small area in the lower back called the epidural space. If there is extensive numbness, it may interfere with the mother's ability to bear down and push, making it necessary to use forceps or vacuum extraction (see page 147) to help guide the baby

out. Serious complications from epidural block are rare. A "walking epidural" is a regional analgesic technique in which a woman maintains strength in her legs. Most patients prefer to stay in bed. Some however, may walk to the bathroom rather than use a bedpan. Being able to retain motor control may help during the second stage of labor. Anesthesiologists skilled in the procedure are able to maximize comfort while having only a minimal effect on your ability to push.

2. *Caudal block:* A local anesthetic is injected into the caudal space located below the tailbone. The effect of a caudal block is the same as with an epidural block. It should be noted that not all women have a caudal space.

3. *Saddle block:* Spinal analgesia usually provides complete pain relief in the "blocked" area. A saddle block is a spinal block in which the level of pain relief is limited to little more than the pelvic region (saddle). Therefore, spontaneous deliveries, operative vaginal deliveries (forceps and vacuum) and episiotomies can be performed using this method of pain relief. Full operative deliveries such as cesarean sections require a higher level and dose of medication (spinal block).

4. *Pudendal block:* This is given shortly before delivery. The drug is injected on either side of the birth canal, numbing the perineum, should it be necessary to perform an episiotomy. It also numbs the area around the vagina and rectum, relieving pain in these areas as the baby descends through the birth canal. Serious side effects from a pudendal block are rare. It is considered one of the safest forms of anesthesia.

5. *Paracervical block:* The injection of a local anesthetic into the tissue on either side of the cervix. Only a very small percentage of vaginal deliveries use this type of anesthetic any longer. Its major drawback is that it slows down the heartbeat of the fetus.

Each of the methods described here has its merits and use in different situations, and there is no one ideal anesthetic for labor and delivery. Because anesthetics, like all drugs, may affect the baby, they must be administered carefully. You will want to discuss the medications and anesthetics available with your clinician to see which one is best for you.

Kinds of Birth

You should now be familiar with the basic process of a "normal" delivery. As the fetus moves down the birth canal, the top of the head becomes visible. This initial view of the head is called crowning. There may or may not be anesthesia administered by the healthcare professional, and in general, nature is allowed to proceed with the unfolding of events, with a little help from medical science. About 90 percent of all deliveries fall into the normal category. The other 10 percent of births fall into one of the following categories.

Breech birth—Instead of the head emerging first, breech-born babies emerge feet and buttocks first. In the "breech" position, the baby prefers to keep his head up out of the birth position. About 3 percent of all babies are breech-born, and clinicians can usually detect the position before the delivery. Such births may require special treatment by the clinician, but in most cases, there is no greater hardship to the mother than in a "normal" delivery, and the baby emerges satisfactorily. Doctors have been using cesarean sections more and more for breech presentations.

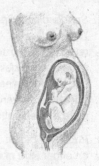

Breech Position

Sometimes the baby can be turned manually into a head-down position. This is called external version, and does not involve surgery. The clinician's hands are placed at certain key points on the lower abdomen. The baby is gently pushed, almost as if baby was doing a somersault in slow motion. The clinician may give you some medication to relax the uterus. External version is done while the clinician watches the fetus with ultrasound.

Forceps delivery—Occasionally, certain physiological conditions make it difficult for a baby to push its head through the birth canal. In that case, the clinician uses a forceps to aid the baby's emergence. The forceps is a curved, tong-like instrument shaped to fit on each side of the baby's head. Sometimes the forceps

Transverse Position

leave a temporary mark on each side of the baby's head, but these marks disappear. There are several advantages to the use of forceps. They can relieve the mother of hours of hard, exhausting labor if her delivery proves stubborn. Forceps may also be necessary when the fetal heart rate slows or becomes irregular. An anesthetic is given prior to the use of forceps.

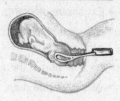

Forceps delivery

Vacuum extraction—The delivery of the baby can also be aided by a method called vacuum extraction. This method is widely used in the U.S. and Europe. It employs a cup-suction device which is applied to the baby's head. The situations when this method would be used are similar to those for a forceps delivery, however, it is contraindicated in preterm delivery.

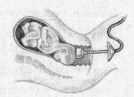

Vacuum extraction

Cesarean birth—A delivery of a baby through the abdomen is called a cesarean birth. In a cesarean, an incision is made in the abdominal wall. This incision may be vertical, extending from the navel to the pubic bone, or it may be transverse, extending from side to side just above the pubic hairline. This is then followed by an incision into the wall of the uterus with the baby delivered through this incision. The incision into the uterus may also be vertical or transverse. The transverse incision is preferred because less blood is lost and the incision heals with a stronger scar. There are situations, however, where a vertical incision may be necessary. The incisions into the uterus and the abdominal wall are closed with sutures following the delivery of the baby and the placenta.

There are a number of reasons why a cesarean birth is indicated. These include:

- Mother's pelvis is too small for passage of the baby.
- Baby is in an abnormal position.
- There are signs the baby is in distress and must be delivered immediately.
- The mother may have medical complications making it necessary to deliver the baby as soon as possible.

- Excessive bleeding.
- Baby's umbilical cord has pushed through the cervix when the membranes ruptured.
- An infection in the amniotic fluid.
- Well past due date.
- Intrauterine growth restriction (page 55).
- Macrosomia (very large baby, page 56).

Cesarean birth is considered major surgery, and though modern surgical techniques have improved greatly, you should be aware of possible risks:

- Hospital stay and recovery time are longer
- Greater loss of blood, sometimes requiring a transfusion
- Infection of pelvic organs
- Infection of incision
- Increased incidence of blood clots in the legs and possibly the lungs
- Impaired bowel function

Should you have any questions or concerns regarding a cesarean birth, feel free to discuss them with your clinician prior to your time of delivery.

Vaginal birth after cesarean (VBAC)

If you have had a cesarean section in a previous birth, can you or should you attempt a vaginal delivery in your next birth? Years ago, there was a principle which said, "once a cesarean section, always a cesarean section." Because the number of cesarean deliveries in the U.S. has increased rapidly, the National Consensus of Cesarean Childbirth did a study to determine whether that old principle is medically sound, or whether a trial of labor for a subsequent delivery is a reasonable alternative. The research shows that at least 60 to 80 percent of women who have had cesarean sections in the past can safely deliver vaginally in subsequent pregnancies.

One factor in determining a vaginal birth after cesarean (VBAC) is the type of incision made in the cesarean. The exact position of a cesarean incision depends on medical considerations, and may be vertical or transverse.

Doctors do advise against a vaginal delivery if a woman has had the classical or fundal vertical cesarean section previously. On the other hand, if a woman has had a low transverse cesarean, she may be advised to undergo a trial of labor for vaginal delivery.

Because there are some risks involved in attempting a vaginal delivery after a previous cesarean(s), several precautionary measures should be taken:

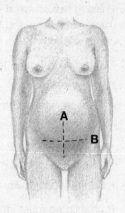

Cesarean birth
A= *Vertical incision*
B= *Transverse incision*

1. It should be a singleton pregnancy (one baby). The previous cesarean should be known to be one with a low transverse uterine incision.

2. Continuous fetal monitoring should be in effect.

3. A physician competent to perform an emergency cesarean should be in the immediate area.

4. Researchers at Harvard Medical School found that women who get pregnant within 9 months of having a C-Section may be at increased risk during an attempted vaginal delivery than are women who wait longer between deliveries.

Women who underwent a cesarean delivery because of a breech position have the best probability of vaginal delivery after a previous C-section. How can you determine whether you are a candidate of VBAC? You and your clinician need to discuss the risks and the benefits to you and your baby of a repeat cesarean, or a trial labor for vaginal delivery. If you choose a trial of labor, it should not be attempted at home.

Preterm labor and delivery

A baby born before 37 weeks' gestation is considered preterm. The smaller and younger the baby, the greater the risk of complications. Although there have been many advances made in this area, preterm births continue to be the most important problem of pregnancy.

Preterm babies are at increased risk for breathing problems, cerebral hemorrhage, infections and feeding problems. Knowing beforehand which factors contribute to preterm delivery may help decrease the risk.

Factors contributing to preterm birth include:

- Poor prenatal care
- A stressful pregnancy
- Past history of miscarriage and/or premature deliveries
- Multiple fetuses
- Smoking
- Uterine abnormality

Probably the most important factor is poor prenatal care. If you believe that you fall into one or more of these categories, or are otherwise at risk, discuss the issue thoroughly with your clinician. Together you can minimize your chances by working out a program for your pregnancy.

However, sometimes, despite all of your precautions, preterm contractions can take you and your clinician by complete surprise. There are times when these contractions start without any pain or forewarning. More frequently though, the first signs are a backache and a tightness around the abdomen.

The FDA has approved a test called a fetal fibronectin assay which helps clinicians decide how to manage patients with symptoms of preterm labor. When the test is negative there is a very low probability that patients will deliver in one or 2 weeks. Although many patients with a positive test will not go into labor, a negative test is very reassuring that the patient is not in actual labor.

If you experience any of the following signs of preterm labor, you should report them to your clinician:

- Lower abdominal pain
- Increased vaginal discharge (may be blood-tinged and watery)
- Low backache
- Abdominal cramps with or without diarrhea
- Regular contractions or tightening sensation

Your clinician may ask you to come to his or her office, or go directly to the hospital, if you have one or more symptoms of premature labor. Tocolytic (to-co-li-tic) agents are drugs used to stop labor. They accomplish this by relaxing the muscles of the uterus. The clinician can administer this medication by injection, in IV fluids, or orally.

Induced labor

Induction of labor refers to the use of certain medications to start labor. The decision to induce labor is usually made by the clinician because of concerns for the mother or fetus, or when the baby is ready to be born and uterine contractions have not begun spontaneously. The initiation of labor through the use of drugs may also be indicated when labor is progressing so slowly that problems might arise for the mother or fetus. The drug most frequently used to induce labor is the intravenous administration of oxytocin.

Labor can also be induced by performing a procedure called an amniotomy. This is the artificial rupturing of the membranes (bag of water). The use of either an amniotomy or intravenous oxytocin to induce labor follows the guidelines of the American College of Obstetricians and Gynecologists.

Fetal Monitoring

Your healthcare provider will be monitoring the condition of your fetus throughout your pregnancy and labor to check on the fetus' status. Because any changes in the heartbeat can signal a possible problem, the clinician monitors the baby's heartbeat frequently and regularly during labor.

Two types of monitoring can be used: auscultation and electronic fetal monitoring.

Auscultation is the term for listening to the heartbeat of the fetus. Most often the clinician uses a Doppler Ultrasound to listen to the heartbeat of the fetus. This instrument uses sound waves to create a signal that is then amplified. The clinician presses the device against the woman's abdomen, and the amplifier makes it possible for anyone in the room to hear the heartbeat.

Another method of listening to the fetal heartbeat is by using a stethoscope-like instrument called a fetoscope. The clinician presses the diaphragm (round flat end) of the fetoscope against the abdomen of the woman. The heartbeat of the fetus can be heard by the one wearing the instrument earpiece.

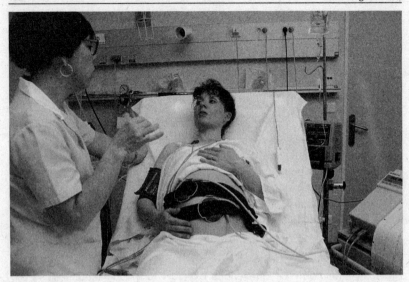

Electronic fetal monitoring measures the heartbeat of the fetus electronically. The heartbeat is recorded continuously and can be read by the clinician. The following are two types of electronic fetal monitoring:

External Monitoring: The clinician places 2 belts around the woman's abdomen. Each belt holds a single instrument in place. One instrument measures fetal heart rate while the other instrument measures both the length of the uterine contractions and the length of time between the contractions.

Internal Monitoring: This method can be administered only after the fetal membranes (bag of water) have broken. The fetal heart rate is recorded by an instrument with an electrode that is attached to the scalp of the fetus. The clinician can also place a thin tube in the uterus to measure the strength of the uterine contractions.

Most women who have had this procedure done report only minor discomfort. Sometimes a clinician will use a combination of internal and external monitoring.

Certified Nurse-Midwives (CNM)

Nurse-midwives attend births in 3 settings: the hospital, at birthing centers and at home. The vast majority of these births (94 percent) are in a hospital setting. The average nurse-midwife has 20 years of clinical experience in maternity and public health. As a growing group of professionals, nurse-midwives are educated in 2 disciplines: nursing and midwifery. The advanced training in midwifery is obtained through accredited programs affiliated with universities across the United States. The American College of Nurse-Midwives certifies graduates by examination and individual license to become Certified Nurse-Midwives (CNM).

Nurse-midwives provide the following:

• Prenatal care

• Labor and delivery

• Postpartum care

• Well-woman gynecology

• Normal newborn care

• Family planning

Nurse-midwives practice in collaboration with physicians. The medical needs of the woman and the practice setting determine the degree of collaboration. The nurse-midwife is especially skilled at risk-screening and will make referrals to a physician's care when necessary.

If you wish to pursue the services of a nurse-midwife and are at low risk for complications during pregnancy, think over the following points:

1. Select one who meets state requirements and has been certified by the American College of Nurse-Midwives (ACNM).

2. To find a nurse-midwife in your area or to check certification, contact the ACNM (8403 Colesville Road, Suite 1550, Silver Springs, MD 20910), or call 240-485-1800 or 1-888-MID-WIFE. Web site: www.midwife.org.

3. Schedule an interview appointment with a nurse-midwife in your area so that you have an opportunity to ask about her services, birth sites, fees and the physician with whom she collaborates if the need arises.

4. Nurse-midwifery care offers women a choice in birth. What is important is that your birth is attended by a caring and appropriate provider of your choice. Prescriptions for medications and vitamins can be written by CNMs.

Nurse-midwifery care is covered by private insurance carriers, Medicare, Medicaid and many managed care programs. CNM services are also covered under the Civilian Health and Medical Program of the Uniformed Services and Federal Employees Health Benefit.

Chapter 14 — After delivery

ODAY, HOSPITAL STAYS FOLLOWING DELIVERY are very short, usually 48 hours (after a vaginal delivery) to 96 hours (after a cesarean section). During your stay, your doctor, as well as the nurses on staff will be available to answer any of your questions about caring for yourself and your baby after you return home. If possible, arrange in advance for someone to help you at home for the first week after you return.

The uterus (womb)

There are many physical changes that occur throughout your body during pregnancy. One of the most remarkable is the change that takes place in your uterus. During the past 9 months this organ has grown, developed, and protected your new baby. Now that you have given birth, your uterus will return to its normal pre-pregnancy size much more rapidly. After delivery the uterus weighs approximately 2½ pounds. By your 6-week checkup, it will weigh only 2 ounces.

After delivery of your baby and the placenta, the nurse massages the uterus to stimulate it to contract. The inability of the uterus to contract is called uterine atony. In this situation, heavy bleeding may occur. If massaging does not work, there are several medications available to the clinician to promote contraction.

As the uterus contracts, there may be occasional abdominal cramps. These are usually more noticeable with a second or third child than with a first. These cramps are called "after pains." With these contractions, the uterus is actually pushing out residual tissue which must be discharged.

This discharge includes the lining of the uterus and other cells that were created for the baby's growth. During the first week, this discharge may be reddish, but by the second week, it may be more brownish. Eventually the discharge becomes paler, fades to yellowish or whitish, and disappears almost completely by the end of the third week. Sometimes, however, it may continue for 6 to 8 weeks before it stops.

The amount of discharge may approximate that of the last day or two of a menstrual period. During this time you should wear a sanitary pad until your clinician advises you otherwise. Do not use a tampon. Regular menstruation will start again in a few weeks if you are not nursing. If you are breastfeeding your baby, it will be much longer before menstruation resumes.

Your breasts

The uterus and the breasts have a close relationship. For example, whether your baby is premature or on time, some unknown internal signal sets off milk production in the breasts 3 days after delivery. The fluid that had been secreted earlier by the breasts was colostrum, the forerunner of the milk.

When the milk is produced there will be several obvious signs, as your breasts will become hard, heavy, full, and uncomfortable. The nursing mother will experience relief from the soreness when the baby begins to suck. For mothers who do not nurse, there may be some discomfort during the period when the milk dries up. To help relieve the discomfort, your clinician may recommend that you wear a tight supportive bra and apply ice packs to your breasts. An analgesic such as acetaminophen may be taken if the tight supportive bra or the ice packs don't relieve your discomfort.

The nursing mother

Almost any woman who decides to breastfeed her baby is able to do so. Breast or nipple size or shape does not affect a mother's ability to nurse her baby.

Your nurse will explain how to place your baby at your breast and demonstrate techniques for keeping baby awake and interested. In order to learn to suck and develop an appetite, the nursing baby will be put to breast a few times before the milk starts to flow. After delivery, your breasts will be secreting the forerunner of breast milk — a yellowish liquid called colostrum. Colostrum contains certain immunological factors that protect a newborn from some types of infections.

If you have the hospital rooming-in plan, you can feed your baby on demand. Let baby nurse 10 to 20 minutes on each breast. The more you nurse the more milk your breasts will produce. As your baby grows, your breasts will automatically accommodate their needs with increased milk production.

The most common and frequently recommended position for breastfeeding is called the "Palmer" grasp. Support the breast with one hand with all the fingers placed under the breast and only the thumb placed above the breast. This positions the breast directly into baby's mouth and avoids having to press the breast away from baby's nose. This grasp is less likely to compress the milk ducts or cut down on the milk flow.

Brush infant's lower lip downward with your nipple, and when infant's mouth opens, insert the nipple and areola in as far as possible. Do not let your baby suck on just the tip or you will get sore nipples. Baby's nose and chin should touch your breast. His lips should be flanged. If the position is uncomfortable, break the suction and begin again.

To stop or interrupt baby during nursing, place your finger in the corner of baby's mouth to open the jaw. This will break the suction between baby's mouth and the nipple/areola and the nipple can be withdrawn.

A nursing mother's nipples do require some extra tender care. Naturally, they must be kept clean. Before nursing, gently wash them with clean water. Allowing them to air dry rather than wiping the nipples with a towel. Absorbent material held in place by your bra may be kept over the nipples between feedings.

You should not be alarmed if your nipples are tender during the first few days of breastfeeding. After lactation has been established and the let-down reflex has occurred, many mothers describe an increase in fluid pressure which is relieved by the infant sucking. As a rule, nipples will adapt naturally to nursing. If, however, pain in your nipples continue, call your clinician or lactation specialist.

In one study of nipple pain, researchers found that the single most important factor was how the breast was presented to the baby. A proper grasp of the breast and correct positioning of the infant, so that baby is facing the breast and baby's body is facing mother's body, is critical to avoiding nipple pain. Baby should not have to turn his head to begin nursing.

If your breasts are sore after nursing, apply an ice pack to your breasts. If you continue to have a problem, contact your clinician or lactation specialist.

The routine use of ointments to the nipples, areola or breast is not recommended. Avoid soaps, alcohol and ointments that contain steroids, antibiotics, astringents or anesthetic agents on your nipples. The anhydrous lanolin, known as Lansinoh, has had all impurities and allergens removed by a special patented process, and is now recommended to relieve nipple soreness and aid in healing.

Because breasts are composed of inelastic ligamentous tissue, not muscle, your genetic makeup will determine how quickly and what shape they will return to. A proper bra to support breasts heavy with milk is important for your comfort and to help minimize sagging. A practical feature of a nursing bra is a handy flap that can open to expose the nipple allowing you to easily feed the baby.

Although the quality of the milk produced by the breast is usually a sweet, rich substance, that milk can be affected by your diet and your medications. Excitement, anxiety or deep depression may also be reflected in the milk's quality. Many drugs taken by the mother are passed on to the baby through the breast milk. Drugs, including laxatives, alcohol, nicotine (from smoking), caffeine, marijuana, and cocaine are all carried in the milk. Even a common drug like aspirin can be transmitted to the baby. Aspirin can affect clotting ability. Consequently, these substances should be eliminated while nursing. If you need to take any drugs, even non-prescription drugs, you should ask your pediatrician.

Remember to alternate the breast you use to begin nursing your baby. That is, if you begin nursing your baby on the left breast, when you nurse for the next feeding, begin with the right breast.

How long should you nurse?

The American Academy of Pediatrics recommends that you nurse your baby for 1 year. Certainly, 6 weeks will give your baby an excellent start, and 2 months or more is even better. The baby will probably signal when he wants to stop nursing, but this will usually not occur for at least 1 year. By then, the need to suck may start to diminish. Weaning is really an individual matter between you and your baby, but as always, your clinician or other healthcare professional can offer practical help.

Women who work outside the home can start breastfeeding until they return to work. Afterwards, part-time breastfeeding can still yield benefits. Some women even arrange babysitting near where they work so that they can nurse in the middle of the day. Breastfeeding is considered by some healthcare providers to be so important that they encourage women to make every effort, even if it is for a short time.

There are 2 additional benefits for the nursing mother. Both the uterus and the abdomen return more quickly to normal in a nursing mother. Also, in most cases, menstruation does not resume until after the baby is weaned. Although, keep in mind, you can still become pregnant while nursing.

The non-nursing mother

Should you decide not to breastfeed your baby, be aware it takes approximately 14 days for the breast glands to stop producing milk. You will probably be advised to wear a tight bra and apply ice packs to your breasts to relieve any discomfort you may have.

Do NOT use a breast pump on your breasts if you are planning not to breastfeed. Pumping your breasts will only cause more milk to be produced.

If you are not breastfeeding, how do you bottle feed your baby? In the hospital, the nurse will supply a warm bottle and will show you how to position both the bottle and the baby. You will hold your baby in your arms with the same closeness of feeling as the nursing mother. A certain amount of patience is necessary to teach the bottle-fed baby how to suck on a nipple. At times, your baby will not get enough milk because the nipple holes are too small. Then you may find in the next feeding that the baby is squirted in the eyes as you bring the bottle near because the hole is too large. It's not unusual to feel frustrated and anxious as the baby cries. You can easily overcome these minor annoyances. The next time you feed, your baby will have forgotten and be sweet, docile, and cooperative. Babies are remarkably resilient.

Smoking and your baby

In a March 8, 1995 issue of The Journal of the American Medical Association, it was reported that even smoking in the same room as an infant increases the risk of sudden infant death syndrome (SIDS). Breastfeeding may protect against SIDS in non-smokers but not in smokers. Researchers have found that breathing someone else's smoke is very dangerous. This is especially true for children.

Environmental tobacco smoke (ETS) is defined as smoke breathed out by a smoker and includes the smoke that comes from the tip of a burning cigarette. ETS has almost 4,000 chemicals in it. According to the American Academy of Pediatrics, infants and children breathe these in whenever someone smokes around them. Children who inhale ETS are at risk for many serious health problems including upper respiratory infections, ear infections and asthma. ETS can also cause problems for children later in life.

Other concerns after delivery

Sterilization

Because sterilization should be viewed as a permanent or irreversible procedure, it is very important that you discuss this option with your partner and give it careful consideration. Among those women who select sterilization as a method of birth control, almost half have it done postpartum (after delivery) in the hospital and usually within a day or two of delivery.

Stitches

If you had an episiotomy, you'll have stitches to close the incision. You may feel them begin to pull and itch by the second day. They may even hurt when you walk or sit. Don't be shy about telling your clinician if your stitches are painful. Your clinician may suggest a sitz bath for relief of discomfort.

Constipation

A common complaint of pregnant women is constipation. Changes in hormones may contribute to the slow movement of food through the digestive tract. Another contributing factor may be a lack of exercise. Pressure exerted on the rectum during labor often causes the rectum to become numb. This may result in the muscles which aid in the expulsion of fecal matter becoming sluggish. The pressure during labor may cause an additional source of discomfort as a few hemorrhoids may be pushed out on the external rectal surface. Your clinician may recommend a stool softener or mild laxative to help you move your bowels without irritating the sore rectal tissues. Other steps you can take to improve regularity include daily exercise, drinking at least eight glasses of liquid a day and eating high-fiber foods such as whole grain cereals and bread, as well as plenty of fruits and vegetables.

Postpartum blues

After delivery, most mothers may expect everything will be fine. And it will be. Still, it's not uncommon at this time to experience mood swings, irritability, fatigue, agitation and symptoms that may indicate depression.

As a new mother, you may not be prepared for some of the typical discomforts or anxieties you are feeling. Your breasts are sore and you are awakened by uterine contractions. You try different positions for sitting and sleeping but still cannot get comfortable. As the baby cries for no apparent reason you feel helpless. Suddenly everything seems to be going wrong and you have to struggle to keep from crying yourself. This emotional storm can be caused by several factors: (1) you feel listless and lacking in energy; (2) your hormones are leveling off to find a new balance; (3) thyroid levels may drop after birth, causing dramatic mood swings; (4) the idea of learning to handle and care for a new baby seems overwhelming; (5) you hurt physically; (6) you may think that your life has changed drastically and that there are so many adjustments you will have to make; (7) you may even feel a sense of loss because you are no longer the pampered pregnant mother who is the center of attention. Instead, the baby is the center of attention and you are merely his or her food source.

One very good outlet for these feelings is talking to other parents—both new and experienced. By sharing your concerns with one another, you can be reassured that the physical and emotional problems that now seem so large will soon be manageable. In most cases, the postpartum blues go away within 2 weeks. If it lasts longer it may be postpartum depression.

Postpartum depression

Approximately 10 percent of mothers develop postpartum depression (PPD).

If after a week or two of the "blues," you are still feeling extreme anxiety, a sense of hopelessness, despair and/or other negative feelings, to the degree that it interferes with your daily life, you may be suffering from postpartum depression. Other symptoms of postpartum depression include:

- Disinterest in your baby or yourself
- Inability to sleep (insomnia) or the wish to sleep all the time even when baby is awake
- Loss of appetite or excessive need to eat all day
- Thoughts of harming yourself or your baby
- Feelings of guilt or hopelessness
- Panic attacks
- Extreme concerns or lack of interest in baby

Should you have any of these signs of postpartum depression, take steps immediately to get the help you need. Speak with your doctor and let him or her know what you are feeling. They have the experience and understanding to support you through this period. If necessary, he or she can refer you to the resources where you can find additional help.

Parenting is a two-person commitment, and the father, who is the closest person to the mother should be able to spot any distress early on. Research has shown that a supportive relationship during PPD treatment is associated with a decline in symptoms of depression. Fathers should look for changes in appetite, extreme anxiety, loss of interest in the baby or other symptoms such as not being able to sleep, or sleeping more than usual. What is important is to be supportive of the new mother and encourage her to seek help.

The majority of these women will develop symptoms of depression by six weeks postpartum and if not treated, many will still be depressed one year after delivery. Early symptoms of depression may occur during the pregnancy. If you have such feelings do not hesitate to discuss this with your clinician. The treatment for postpartum depression as well as during pregnancy is highly successful once the disorder is diagnosed and treatment is begun.

Postpartum psychosis is the most severe type of postpartum depression. It occurs rapidly over a 24- to 72-hour period, and usually begins several days postpartum, with the greatest risk occurring within the first month after delivery. Symptoms of postpartum psychosis may include the symptoms of depression along with symptoms of extreme confusion, disorientation and distractibility. Prompt referral for medical/psychological evaluation and treatment is essential.

If your postpartum blues last longer than a couple of weeks, or your negative feelings become worse instead of better, call your doctor or other health-care professional for help. Postpartum depression and its debilitating effects can affect the entire family. There are hotlines and support groups that may be helpful. Your clinician can refer you to resources in your area.

Remember, the treatment for postpartum depression is highly successful once the disorder is diagnosed and treatment is begun.

Circumcision for baby boys

Circumcision, one of the oldest known surgical procedures, is the practice of removing the foreskin from the penis of baby boys. In recent decades, medical views about the health benefits of circumcision have changed.

Though some studies have reported uncircumcised males may have a higher incidence of sexually transmitted diseases and the circumcision may provide some degree of protection against disease, the validity of these medical arguments has been questioned as new information becomes available. The American Academy of Pediatrics currently views circumcision, not as a medical decision, but rather as one of parental choice. Circumcision is not required by law or hospital policy. It is performed at the request of the parents.

More evidence is now accumulating supporting the position that circumcision does offer protection against urinary tract infections, as well as cervical cancer in female partners, genital ulcer disease and HIV infection. Complications following circumcision are rare and almost always minor according to a recent article.

Some parents want their sons circumcised for religious or cultural reasons. If there are no contraindications, the procedure is usually performed by the doctor before the baby leaves the hospital. The penis heals within a week. Very rarely are there complications.

Discuss circumcision with your doctor or other healthcare professional long before your due date so that you can make an informed decision.

Visitors

On average, your hospital stay after a vaginal delivery will last from 1 to 2 days. During that time, many hospitals have opportunities for new mothers to participate in demonstrations on bathing, feeding and caring for your new infant. Or you may be able to watch a movie on these subjects. While in the hospital it's your decision whether or not you want to have visitors. Whatever you decide, it is important that you rest as much as possible. If you do have visitors, you will need to take into account the hospital's visiting rules. These rules vary among hospitals. The times for visiting hours are for the good of the patient and the efficiency of the hospital. In some facilities they may be restricted to 1 or 2 hours. There may also be a limit on the number of visitors allowed in a room at one time.

A few pointers about hygiene

A sponge bath at your bedside or sink will have to suffice until your doctor feels you are strong enough to take a tub bath or shower.

Use soft tissues or cotton balls to wipe yourself following urination and bowel movements. Remember, always wipe from front (vagina) to back, toward the anus (rectum)—never wipe from back to front. This is to help avoid introducing foreign bacteria into the vagina. Always put on a clean sanitary pad after using the toilet. The hospital will provide you with pads during your stay. Soiled pads should be discarded in bags specially provided for this purpose.

Chapter 15 Going home

*Y*OUR HOSPITAL STAY WILL GO BY VERY QUICKLY, usually only 1 or 2 days. Before you know it you will be getting ready to go home. So much has taken place during the past few days in the hospital that it may seem incredible that you are returning home with a new infant in your arms and a dramatically changed body.

The baby's clothes that you packed in your overnight case will be brought to you, and one of the nurses will help you dress your baby for the trip home. How many and what kind of clothes and blankets the baby needs depends on the weather conditions on the day of discharge.

If you have arranged any household help, that person should be ready and waiting for your arrival. When you first return home, it is probably a good idea to lie down and rest. Though you've been looking forward to going home, remember that your routine will change considerably with the new baby. Don't be too eager to jump back in to your regular household chores.

Family members may want to come over and welcome you back, but for your sake and the baby's, it is probably best to postpone their visits for a day or two. Your baby will be adjusting to the surroundings and will be under some strain. Too much activity as well as loud, sharp noises may frighten the baby. This can make it even more difficult for him or her to settle-in as a new member of your family.

Postpartum exercises

Though you may have now lost the large abdomen, one glance in a full-length mirror will tell you that you are still a long way from your pre-pregnancy size. Your previous wardrobe will still be too tight to zip or button up. Expectations of returning immediately to non-maternity clothes are just not realistic.

The best way to get back in shape is exercise. It is important to exercise not only so that you will look better, but also to tighten and tone the muscles that were stretched during your pregnancy.

Ask your doctor how soon you can begin your postpartum exercises. Unless contraindicated, begin with simple exercises while you are in the hospital, exercising just once or twice a day, increasing gradually, and stoping before you become fatigued or strain a muscle. You should also resume the Kegel exercises described on page 89 as soon as you are able. These exercises will stimulate the flow of blood to the pelvic floor and thus promote healing.

First week exercises

For leg raises, lie flat on your back. Raise the right foot off the bed about 6 inches, keeping the left slightly bent. Lower the right leg slowly. Do the same with the left leg. Alternate the legs. Repeat 4 to 5 times.

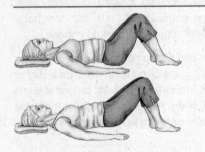

For tightening the abdominal muscles lie on your back with your head on pillow. Bend knees and keep feet flat on the floor or bed. Arch your back and push your seat against the floor. Then push your back against the floor and raise your pelvic area. Contract abdominal muscles. Relax and begin again. Repeat 4 or 5 times at first.

This exercise will help your uterus return to a good position. Lie stomach down, palms up, a folded blanket or pillow under your hips and another under your ankles. Turn your face to one side and fall asleep if you can during this "exercise."

Second week exercises

This exercise helps the uterus to return to its normal size and position. Keep your forehead on the floor. Lean on your elbows and knees and arrange them so they are together. Pull your back upward, contract your buttocks, and pull in your abdomen. Relax and breathe deeply. Try to assume this position every morning and evening for about 5 minutes.

For abdominal muscle tone, get down on your hands and knees with feet slightly apart, head parallel to the floor. Gently pull in abdominal muscles and round your back like a cat. Hold for a second, then let the abdominal muscles sag completely, hollowing the back. Repeat several times.

Third week exercises

Walking is still one of the best exercises. About the beginning of the 3rd week, you can take a walk out of doors, but do make an effort to do a lot of walking about the house before then. Walk with the abdomen pulled in, chin high, and swing the arms.

For trunk muscles, get on hands and knees keeping the back as straight as possible. Turn your head to the right and look toward your feet. As you turn, contract your right trunk muscles and stretch the left ones. Straighten the body, rest a minute, then repeat in the opposite direction.

Fourth week exercises

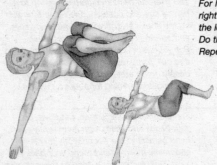

For leg raises, lie flat on your back. Raise the right foot off the bed about 6 inches, keeping the left slightly bent. Lower the right leg slowly. Do the same with the left leg. Alternate the legs. Repeat 4 to 5 times.

Swimming

Swimming is very helpful in regaining abdominal muscle tone. Increase time gradually and adjust to your capacity. Do not rush your schedule.

Exercise for your breasts

Breasts have no muscle tissue, they are formed of glands and fatty tissue. Exercise of any kind cannot firm them up. However, the prominence and contour of the breasts are helped by strengthening the pectoral muscles upon which the breasts rest.

With arms semi-outstretched, place your hands together while opposing each other and push firmly. This isometric exercise causes the pectoral muscles to stand out.

Diet

Write down your ideal weight and body measurements. Now take your present weight and measurements and compare them with your ideal numbers. How close are these 2 sets of measurements?

The only way to lose weight is to consume fewer calories than your body burns. A non-nursing woman burns about 2,000 calories a day. Nutritious, lower calorie meals coupled with a conscientiously followed exercise program will enable you to lose weight rapidly. In about 2 months, you should be back to your pre-pregnancy weight. Before leaving the hospital check with your nurse for information on nutritious, low-calorie postnatal meals.

Return of menstruation

The role of the uterus was discussed in Chapter 14. The uterus returns to its normal size in approximately 6 weeks. If you are not nursing, your menstrual period may resume 7 to 9 weeks after delivery, although it is not unusual for it to take a little longer. Your first period may be somewhat erratic, lasting for a longer or shorter period of time than is usual for you. It may also be heavier or lighter than you've experienced in the past. Your system will regulate itself in a month or two and return to what is normal for you. It is not unusual for women who suffered from severe menstrual cramps (dysmenorrhea) before becoming pregnant to experience less discomfort during menstruation after the baby is born.

If you are breastfeeding your baby, your menstrual periods may be delayed for several months or possibly not resume until you stop breastfeeding. It is still possible, however, to get pregnant while you are nursing your baby. Breastfeeding is not a reliable form of birth control.

Sex relations and family planning

A few weeks after delivery, you will need to see your clinician for a postpartum checkup. It is often a good idea to refrain from sexual relations until after this checkup. The reason is that your internal organs are still sensitive. You may be sore, and your uterus is still in the process of shrinking. You will probably also be experiencing some vaginal discharge.

Although the postpartum period lasts for 6 weeks, many couples resume sexual relations before it is over. The resumption of sexual relations is neither harmful nor dangerous, depending on your physical condition and frame-of-mind. Remember, you are not immune from pregnancy during the postpartum period. If you are going to resume a sexual relationship, you should use a reliable form of contraception, provided you have no religious or moral objections to birth control devices. If you used a diaphragm or a cervical cap prior to your pregnancy and wish to continue to use either of these forms of contraception again, you must be re-measured since most frequently there is a size change following delivery.

The postpartum period is also a good time to discuss with your partner your plans for other babies. You and your husband need to decide how you want your babies to be spaced. You must allow your body time to regain its strength and give your reproductive organs a rest before you conceive again. It will take about 3 months for you to feel more like you did before becoming pregnant. For most women, a wait of 1 1/2 to 2 years between births is best.

Emergency contraception

If you and your partner have engaged in unprotected sex, contact your health-care professional right away to discuss emergency contraception. A high dosage of birth control pills taken within 72 hours of sex, followed by a second dose 12 hours later, lowers the risk of pregnancy by approximately 75 percent. Another emergency contraception protocol is to have your clinician insert an IUD after unprotected sex. Emergency contraception works by preventing ovulation, preventing a fertilized egg from implanting in the uterus or blocking fertilization. The high dose of birth control pills may cause nausea, bloating and breast tenderness for a day or two. If you do not get your period within 3 weeks, take a home pregnancy test and contact your physician.

If you have any questions or concerns about either resumption of sexual relations or birth control, be sure to discuss them with your clinician.

Your postpartum check-up

This examination will be similar to your original examination for pregnancy. However, this time your clinician will be checking other factors. He or she wants to make sure all your organs have resumed their normal size and position, any vaginal stitches have dissolved, and the cervix has healed. The clinician may also examine your breasts. Nursing mothers may be asked to return after they have weaned their babies.

Even if you are not pregnant you should plan on yearly visits to your doctor. Annual gynecological exams are a vital part of women's health. Clinicians routinely use the Pap test, a simple but highly effective method for detecting the presence of abnormal cells in the cervix. A tiny smear of vaginal secretion is examined through a microscope. The abnormal appearance of cells in the specimen may indicate the presence of a precancerous or cancerous condition. With early detection, treatment can be more effective.

Signs and symptoms to report after delivery

- Fever over 100.4°F (38°C)
- Bleeding heavier than a menstrual period
- Swelling and tenderness in your legs
- Chest pain and/or cough
- Nausea and vomiting
- Burning, pain, urgency (frequent, strong desire to void) on urination
- Painful, hot and tender breasts
- Perineal pain and tenderness that does not subside

Some advice about your first weeks at home

1. It is a good idea to stay around the house for the first week or so.
2. One nap a day is desirable, two if possible.
3. Consult with your clinician about how soon you can drive a car.
4. If you are not nursing your baby and your breasts are having trouble drying up, use ice packs. Ask your clinician about medication if your breasts become painful.
5. In a few weeks, you may again experience baby "blues." You are especially likely to become cross and irritable if you allow yourself to become overtired. However, this condition is perfectly normal. You will know when it is happening to you, and you will know that it passes.
6. Before you attempt to get pregnant again, it is a good idea to give your body a few months to rest. During this time, your body can rebuild its store of nutrients.

Chapter 16 Working at motherhood

*B*EING A MOTHER PROVIDES A GREAT DEAL OF PLEASURE, but also requires a great deal of work. It is important to know ahead of time about some of the circumstances that will occur in the first few weeks and months of motherhood.

Baby's weight

The first week after bringing your baby home, you may notice that your baby looks thinner than at birth. Your first reaction may be to question whether or not you're feeding him or her enough.

Don't worry, it's not unusual for babies to lose weight during their first week of life. Your baby will be back to their birth weight in another week, and after that will continue to grow rapidly.

Baby's sleeping position

The American Academy of Pediatrics now recommends that all healthy infants be placed on their backs to sleep rather than on their stomachs. Unless there are special medical conditions requiring your baby to sleep on his or her stomach, always put your baby to sleep on his/her back. If special conditions exist, discuss the situation with your physician before placing your baby to sleep on his/her stomach. Studies have found that infants who sleep on their stomachs have a higher incidence of sudden infant death syndrome (SIDS). While awake and under your watchful eyes, you can allow your baby play time on his/her stomach.

The soft spot

When observing your baby closely, you will notice what looks like a soft spot at the top of the head. This soft spot is known as a fontanelle. This skeletal separation of the baby's skull allows the head to conform to the shape of the vaginal canal during delivery. After birth, the head may even look quite elongated rather than round. In a few months, this will change as the head rounds out and the fontanelle begins to close. By 2 years of age, this soft spot will be completely closed. You must take added precautions that your baby does not fall or receive blows to the head that would cause serious and permanent injury. It is perfectly safe to wash baby's head when he/she is being bathed.

You shouldn't be alarmed if you see some black and blue marks on your baby's head after delivery. The forces of labor put a great deal of pressure on the baby's head. Forceps or vacuum delivery can also leave bruises. These black and blue marks usually disappear in a couple of days.

Jaundice

About 2 to 5 days after birth, the baby's skin takes on a yellow-orange tinge. This is called physiologic jaundice of the newborn and occurs in about 1/3 of all babies. The jaundice is caused by an increase in the concentration of bilirubin in the baby's blood. Bilirubin is made up of by-products of hemoglobin from the baby's red blood cells. Normally these by-products are disposed of through the liver and kidneys. Sometimes, especially in preterm babies, the baby's liver is not yet fully mature. Feeding the newborn soon after birth may help to decrease the risk of jaundice. The feeding ensures the baby is well hydrated and stimulates the baby's digestive tract.

If the bilirubin is high enough, or the jaundice lasts longer than usual or occurs very early, the baby's doctor may want to start therapy. This involves placing the baby under special phototherapy lights. The lighting helps breakup the bilirubin so that it can be excreted more quickly.

Caring for the umbilical cord and circumcision

When your baby was born, the clinician severed the umbilical cord and now a small stump remains attached to the baby's navel. The first day or two after birth, this stump will begin to shrivel and start to dry up. Sometime between the 7th and 8th day, it will drop off. Until it does drop off, it will be attached to the baby. You should simply allow nature to take its course. When bathing the baby, you should keep the area clean by removing crusty material. If necessary, you can use baby oil to soften the crusty area.

The circumcision heals naturally and complications following a circumcision are rare. After the procedure is completed, the penis is wrapped with a gauze square saturated with vaseline or other suitable cream. The gauze usually falls off the penis by itself. If it does not fall off, do not pull on it, just squeeze some warm water on the gauze to loosen it. Check with your clinician as to the care of the circumcised or uncircumcised penis.

Birth certificate

Every baby born in the United States and Canada must be registered at birth. Your physician will sign a birth certificate that will be filed with the appropriate agency in your city or town. You will receive a certified copy of it about 4 weeks after the birth. Check it carefully for accuracy as soon as it arrives. Be sure the

To request the form needed to apply for a social security number for your baby call:
800-772-1213

names are spelled correctly and the dates are right. If any information is wrong you should have it corrected at once. Place the birth certificate somewhere that is safe. It is also a good idea to have a copy made. This certificate will be needed when your child registers for school as well as for other occasions.

Enjoy your baby

Learn to enjoy your role as a new parent now that your baby is off to a good start in life. Reading books and articles on childcare can help you reduce many of the fears or anxieties you may have about raising your baby. They will help you know what to expect at different steps in your baby's development. Your doctor will help you with information on how frequently your baby needs to be examined, when immunization programs must be started, and any other important issues about your baby's development and health.

Pregnancy Appendix

What to do in an emergency childbirth

Late in pregnancy, expectant mothers taking trips should make certain that appropriate medical care is nearby. If possible, you should ask your clinician for the names of colleagues in the area where you'll be traveling. At other times, pregnant mothers and their families may go camping or take boating trips to isolated areas, increasing their chances of delivering the baby on their own.

The following are step-by-step guidelines for emergency childbirth recommended by leading experts. Most of the advice is directed to the father. However, the mother should also be acquainted with these steps and be fully prepared for an emergency.

1. Attempt to get help. Contact your clinician and call for an ambulance if going to the hospital on your own isn't possible. If there is no way of getting to the hospital in time don't panic. This rule applies to both parents.

2. Keep calm. Remember, pregnancy is a normal condition, and childbirth is the natural culmination of that process.

3. Help make the mother comfortable. A pregnant woman who is about to deliver will be most comfortable and safe when lying down. Place her on a bed, a floor (in a camper), or on the seat of a car. Depending on the time available, you should place paper or a clean sheet or towel underneath her in order to absorb the excess fluid expelled during delivery. If the mother prefers, however, she can sit up or even assume a squatting position. At this time, the mother should practice her prenatal relaxation exercises. If the mother has an urge to empty her bladder or bowel, she should use a bedpan or a basin. She should not use the toilet.

4. Thoroughly wash your hands. Use plenty of soap and water to help prevent infection. Do not try to clean any area of the mother's body, including the vaginal entrance.

5. Allow the baby to come out naturally. When the baby enters the birth canal, nature will prevail, forcing the mother to bear down until the baby is delivered. During labor, the mother should try to relax, breathing as normally as possible. If the mother becomes tense, the contractions will be less effective in dilating the cervix and delivery may be delayed. You may hear the mother scream if her contractions are extremely painful. Don't let her screams upset you. Keep calm. The father should not pull, push, tug or interfere in any way with the delivery. The baby should then be allowed to emerge onto a clean towel or sheet. Sometimes in bearing down, the mother may have a bowel movement. Take the feces and cover or remove it to avoid contaminating the baby.

   If you were unable to reach your healthcare provider and trouble develops, you should help the mother to lie down or place her in the most comfortable position in your car, and take her to the nearest help available.

6. If the baby emerges in the unbroken sac, you should break that sac. Usually the sac will already have broken spontaneously. If not, carefully use your fingernail, a pin, or other sharp object to break it open. Warning: be very careful not to injure the baby inside the sac. Once the sac is broken, wipe the sac away from the baby's head so that normal breathing can start.

7. Clean off the baby's face, using a clean handkerchief, towel, or even a clean T-shirt if nothing else is available. Do not use paper towels. Paper towels can tear and small pieces could become lodged in the baby's nostrils or mouth then inhaled into the lungs. Using the towel, gently wipe the baby's face and head, including the nose and mouth. Wiping off the baby's face will be remove any thick mucus that could be inhaled into the baby's lungs.

8. Be careful with the umbilical cord. After the baby emerges, the cord should be left slack, especially if it is still pulsating, to allow the blood to continue flowing to the baby. The umbilical cord extends from the baby's navel to the afterbirth. During pregnancy, this is the baby's lifeline for food

and oxygen. Make sure that the cord is not wrapped around the baby's neck. You do not have to cut the cord immediately after the baby is born. When the clinician arrives later, he or she can do this. However, if no medical assistance is available, you should take a piece of clean string or strong twine and tie the cord tightly in two places. Then take a pair of clean scissors or a knife and cut the cord between the two ties.

9. Do not dispose of the afterbirth. Usually the afterbirth, which is attached to the umbilical cord, will be expelled from the mother without assistance. You should not pull on the umbilical cord to remove the afterbirth because you might prematurely break the cord. When the afterbirth emerges, you should place it in a basin or on a newspaper. The clinician will want to examine it to make sure nothing has been left inside the mother.

10. Place the baby as close to the mother as possible. The mother's body is the best place to keep the baby warm. If you find that the umbilical cord is long enough, you should place the baby on the mother's arm or next to her breast. Whether or not nursing takes place, it will actually help the mother if the baby sucks at her nipple. The sucking causes the uterus to contract, which helps expel the afterbirth more quickly. If you find that the umbilical cord is short, remove or cover the fluid between the mother's legs and place the baby there.

11. Place a cover over the baby. If nothing else is available, use a warm blanket or coat. The top of the baby's head should also be covered because the baby can lose a great deal of body heat through their head. Be careful not to block the baby's mouth and nose so that he or she can breathe normally.

12. Begin massaging the mother's abdomen where the uterus is located. This will help prevent excessive bleeding even if the afterbirth has been expelled. Locate the uterus by placing a cupped hand just between the pubic hair and the belly button.

13. Complete the delivery by cleaning the mother and making her warm and comfortable. However, do not attempt to clean the baby. The cheesy coating on the skin protects the baby, and should be allowed to remain for a while. Make sure the baby is warm. While you and the mother are waiting for the clinician, try to relax and enjoy your success.

The appearance of a healthy week-old baby.

THE LEGS are most often seen drawn up against the abdomen in pre-birth position. Extended legs measure shorter than you'd expect compared to the arms. The knees stay slightly bent and legs are more or less bowed.

THE FACE will disappoint you unless you are expecting pudgy cheeks, a broad, flat nose with the mere hint of a bridge, receding chin and undersized lower jaw.

WEIGHT unless well above the average of 7 or 8 lb you'll be surprised by how really tiny a newborn is. Top to toe measure is anywhere between 19 and 21 inches.

ON THE SKULL you will see or feel the two most obvious soft spots or fontanelles. One is above the brow, the other close to crown of head in back.

A DEEP FLUSH spreads over the entire body if the baby cries hard. Veins on the head swell and throb. Because the tear ducts are not functioning yet, you will notice there are no tears when the baby cries.

THE FEET look more complete than they are. X-ray would show only one real bone of the heel. Other bones are now cartilage. Skin is often loose and wrinkly.

THE TRUNK may startle you with the short neck, small sloping shoulders, swollen breasts, large rounded abdomen, umbilical stump (future navel) and slender, narrow pelvis and hips.

THE SKIN is thin and dry. You may see veins through it. Fair skin may be temporarily rosy-red. Downy hair is not unusual.

EYES appear dark blue with a blank starry gaze. You may catch one or both turning or turned to crossed or wall-eyed position.

THE HANDS, if you open them out flat from their characteristic fist position, have finely lined palms, tissue-paper thin nails, dry loose fitting skin and deep bracelet creases at the wrist.

GENITALS of both sexes will seem large (especially the scrotum) in comparison with the scale of, for example, the hands to adult size.

THE HEAD usually strikes you as being too big for the body. Immediately after birth it may be temporarily out of shape, lop-sided or elongated due to pressure before or during birth.

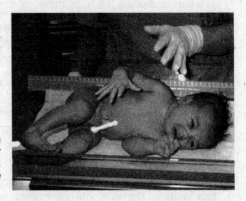

Agents known to be harmful to the fetus

Agent	Why or how used	Effects on the fetus
Accutane	Cystic acne.	Abnormalities during the developmental stage. Increases risk of miscarriage.
Alcohol	Social reasons, dependency.	Mental retardation. Abnormal growth pattern. Fetal Alcohol syndrome (FAS).
Androgens	To treat endometriosis.	Genital abnormalities.
Anticoagulants	Prevent blood clotting. To treat thromboembolism (clots that can block blood vessel).	Increased risk of bleeding. Abnormalities in bones, cartilage and eyes. Possible central nervous systems defects.
Antithyroid drugs	To treat hyperthyroidism.	Enlarged or underactive thyroid condition.
Anticonvulsants	To treat epilepsy.	Mental and physical growth retardation, developmental abnormalities and neural tube defects (spina bifida or anencephaly).
Chemotherapy	To treat cancer or severe psoriasis (a skin condition). Topical agents used to treat psoriasis should be avoided.	Increase in incidences of miscarriage and birth defects.
Diethylstilbestrol (DES)	Used in the 1940's and 1950's to help prevent miscarriages and preterm labor. Used in treating problems with menstruation, menopause and breast cancer. Also used to stop the production of millk.	Abnormal changes in the cervix and uterus of the female fetus. Possible effect on male and female fertility.
Isotretinoin	See Accutane	
Lead	Used in manufacturing products such as paint, printing ink, glass, electronic components, ceramics and pottery glazing.	Increased incidence of stillbirths and miscarriage.
Lithium	To treat depression.	Congenital heart defects.
Mercury (Organic)	Environmental contamination found in fish and possibly other foods.	Brain disorders.
Soriatane	Topical agent used to treat psoriasis.	Abnormal changes in the cervix and uterus of female fetus. Possibility of male and female infertility.
Streptomycin	An antibiotic for treating tuberculosis or other infections.	Hearing loss.
Tetracycline	An antibiotic for treating various types of infections.	Affects development of tooth enamel.
Thalidomide	Once used as a sedative to treat sleep disorders and "morning sickness."	Limb reduction, absence of limb.
X-ray therapy	To treat medical disorders including cancer.	Retardation. Developmental abnormalities in mental or physical growth.

Family Medical History

Detailed family medical records are helpful in diagnosing and treating potential health problems, especially those that recur in some families. For your clinician's reference, note any serious diseases in your family. The list below should be consulted when filling out the form. When you have completed the form, discuss it with your clinician.

Is there any history in your family of:

Allergies	Hearing defects	Sickle cell anemia
Arthritis	Heart defects	Tay-Sachs disease
Cancer	Hemophilia	Visual defects
Diabetes	Hypertension	Other recurring family
Epilepsy	Mental retardation	diseases

Relationship	Birth date	Blood type and Rh	Disease History	Medications
Mother				
Her mother				
Her father				
Father				
His mother				
His father				
Siblings				

Comparative Prenatal Weight Gain Chart

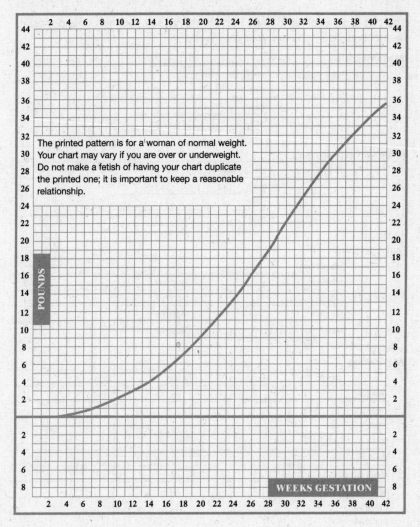

The printed pattern is for a woman of normal weight. Your chart may vary if you are over or underweight. Do not make a fetish of having your chart duplicate the printed one; it is important to keep a reasonable relationship.

POUNDS

WEEKS GESTATION

Your Weight Chart

You can use this chart to keep track of changes in your weight and measurements during and after your pregnancy.

Before Pregnancy

Ideal weight	Ideal measurements:
	bust
	waist
	hips

At the start of pregnancy

Weight	Measurements:
	bust
	waist
	hips

During pregnancy

Weight gain	
Month 2	Month 6
Month 3	Month 7
Month 4	Month 8
Month 5	Month 9

After delivery

	Weight	Bust	Waist	Hips
Week 1				
Week 2				
Week 3				
Week 4				
Week 5				
Week 6				
Month 2				
Month 3				
Month 4				
Month 5				
Month 6				

Calorie counter

The calories listed are average amounts, and although the caloric content of individual foods may vary, your diet should average to the correct number of calories if you use the listed figures. Bear in mind that your diet must supply enough of all of the important food elements: vitamins, minerals, proteins, etc. The best diet is the one your clinician recommends. Be sure you follow it.

Calories in one gram of:	carbohydrate	4 calories
	fat	9 calories
	protein	4 calories

T. = Tablespoon

Calories

A

Almonds (1-1/2 cup)	424
Angel food cake (2" slice)	108
Apple (1 average size)	76
Apple juice (1 cup)	124
Apple pie (4" slice)	331
Applesauce, sweetened (1 cup)	184
Apricot (1 large)	18
canned in syrup (4 halves + 2 T. juice)	97
dried (1 half)	10
Asparagus (6 spears)	22
Asparagus soup, creamed (1 cup)	200
Avocado (1/2 med. size)	279

B

Bacon, Canadian, fried (1 slice)	50
Banana (1 large)	119
Beans baked (1/3 cup)	108
green (1/3 cup)	9
kidney (1/3 cup)	76
lima-young, fresh	50
Bean soup (1 cup)	191
Beef:	
pot roast (1 slice)	200
prime rib (1 slice)	200
steak (1 serving)	300
Beef and vegetable stew (1 cup)	252
Beets (1/3 cup)	23

Berry pie (1 slice)	350
Berries:	
Blackberries	
canned in syrup (1/3 cup)	72
fresh (1/3 cup)	27
Blueberries (1/3 cup)	28
canned in syrup (1/3 cup)	82
water packed (1/3 cup)	30
Raspberries, black, fresh (1/3 cup)	33
red, fresh (1/3 cup)	23
frozen (3 oz. pkg.)	85
water-packed (1/3 cup)	33
Strawberries, fresh (1/2 cup)	27
frozen (3 oz.)	100
Biscuits, baking powder (1)	129
Bologna (1 slice)	116
Bouillion (1 cup)	9
Bread:	
Cracked wheat (1 slice)	60
French (1 slice)	50
Raisin (1 slice)	65
Rye (1 slice)	57
White (1 slice)	64
Whole wheat (1 slice)	55
Broccoli (1/3 cup)	17
Brownies (one)	100
Buns, hamburger (one)	150
Butter (1 average pat)	50

C

Candy, hard (one piece)	36
Cantaloupe (1/2)	37
Carbonated beverages (cola-type) (1 glass)	105
Carrots (1/3 cup)	15
Cashew nuts (1 oz.)	164
Catsup (1 T.)	17
Cauliflower, cooked (1/3 cup)	10
Cereals, cooked (1/3 cup)	55

Corn meal
Cream of Wheat
Farina
Hominy Grits
Rolled Oats
Wheat, whole

Cereals, dry:

Bran Flakes (1 cup)	117
Corn Flakes (1 cup)	96
Grape Nuts (1 T.)	28
Rice, puffed (1 cup)	39
Rice flakes (1 cup)	39
Rice Krispies (1 cup)	133
Shredded Wheat (1 large size)	100

Cheese:

Blue (1 oz.)	104
Camembert (1 oz.)	85
Cheddar (1 oz.)	113
Cottage (1/3 cup)	90
Cream (1 T.)	56
Edam (1" cube)	100
Limburger (1 oz.)	97
Roquefort (1 oz.)	104
Swiss (1 oz.)	105

Cherries, canned in syrup (1/3 cup)	40
Chestnuts (one)	5

Chicken:

breast, roasted (1 slice)	50
broiled (1 average piece)	50
canned, boned (1/3 cup)	200
liver (one)	50
Chicken soup or consomme (1 cup)	75
noodle soup (1 cup)	150
with rice soup (1 cup)	100
Chicken salad (1/3 cup)	133

Chili sauce (1 T.)	17

Chocolate bar, milk, plain (1 oz.)	143
with almonds (1 oz.)	151
Chocolate cake (1 slice)	150
Chocolate creams (one)	100
Chocolate fudge sauce (1 T.)	100
Chocolate milk (1 cup)	185
Chocolate chip cookies (1)	75
Chocolate syrup (1 T.)	42
Chop suey, meat and vegetables (1 cup)	200
Cider (1 cup)	124
Clams (4 oz.)	92
Clam chowder (1 cup)	200
Coconut cake with icing (1 average slice)	150
Coffee, black	0
with sugar or cream (1 cup)	100
Coffee cake (1 slice)	100
Cole slaw (1/3 cup)	34
Collards (1/3 cup)	25
Cookie, plain (one)	100
Corn, canned (3 oz.)	56
on cob (one ear)	84
Corn bread or muffin (one)	159
Cooking oil (1 T.)	125
Crab meat (1/2 cup)	50
salad (1/3 cup)	40

Crackers:

Graham (1 small)	14
Matzoth (one)	100
Pretzel (one)	17
Ry-Krisp (one)	20
Saltines (1 double)	33
Soda (one)	17

Cranberries (1/3 cup)	18
sauce (1/3 cup)	208
Cream, light (1 T.)	30
sour, heavy (1 T.)	49
whipped (1 T.)	50
Cream puff (one)	150
Cream sauce (1 T.)	33
Cucumber, raw (1 slice)	1
Cup cake, iced (one)	200
Cup cake, plain (one)	150
Custard pie (1 slice)	266
Pudding (1/3 cup)	100

Marshmallows (one)...20
Mayonnaise (1 T.)...100
Melba toast (1 slice)..25
Milk:
   Buttermilk, cultured (1 glass)........................86
   Skim (1 glass)..87
   Whole (1 glass) 166
   Skim, powdered (1 T.)................................33
   Whole, powdered (1 T.)..............................40
Minced pie (1 slice)...341
Mints, chocolate (one) 50
Molasses (1 T.)...45
Muffins (one)..134
Mushrooms, canned (1/3 cup) 9
   soup, creamed (1 cup) 300

N

Nectarine, fresh (one) 100
Noodles (and spaghetti), cooked 107
   (1 cup)

O

Oatmeal cookies, plain (1) 50
Olive, green (one) 7
Olive oil (1 T.)........................... 125
Onions, raw (one) 50
   small, green (one)....................... 4
Onion soup (1 cup)........................ 100
Orange, fresh (1 large) 106
Orange juice, frozen 300
   Concentrate (6 oz. can) ....
Orange juice, fresh or canned,........... 108
   unsweetened (1 glass).....................
Ovaltine, skim milk (1 glass)............ 120
Oxtail soup (1 cup) 200
Oysters, raw (one)........................ 14
Oyster soup, creamed (1 cup) 100
   stew, 6-8 oysters (1 cup).............. 250

P

Pancakes (one) 59
Parsley (1 T.) 1
Parsnips, boiled (1 cup) 94
Peaches, canned in syrup (2 halves)....... 79
   fresh (one) 46
   frozen (4 oz.)......................... 89
Peanuts, shelled, roasted (1 T.) 50

Peanut brittle (1 piece) 50
Peanut butter (1 T.) 92
Pears, fresh (one) 95
   syrup packed (1/3 cup) 58
   water packed (1/3 cup) 25
Peas, canned (1/3 cup)................... 48
   fresh or frozen (1/3 cup) 37
Pea soup (1 cup)........................ 141
Pecans (1 T.) 52
Peppers (one) 16
Pepper-pot soup (1 cup)................ 250
Pickles, dill, large (one) 15
   sweet (one)............................ 22
   relish, sweet (1 T.) 15
Pineapple, canned in syrup 95
   (1 slice + juice)
   fresh (1 slice) 44
   frozen (4 oz.)......................... 97
   juice, canned (1 glass) 121
Pistachio nuts (1 T.)................... 33
Plums (one) 29
Plum pudding (1 slice) 200
Popcorn, plain (popped) (1 cup)........ 54
Pork chop (1 serving) 310
Pork roast (1 slice) 350
Pork sausage (one)..................... 75
Postum (1 cup) 6
Potatoes, baked (one)................. 97
   boiled (one) 118
   French fries (one).................... 18
   fried (1/3 cup)....................... 160
   hash brown (1/3 cup).................. 157
   mashed (1/3 cup)...................... 53
   new (one) 25
   sweet, baked (one) 200
   canned (1/3 cup) 75
Potato chips (one).................... 11
Potato salad (1/3 cup)................ 66
Potato soup (1 cup) 200
Pound cake (1 slice) 200
Pretzel (one)......................... 4
Prunes, dried (one) 20
   sweetened (1/3 cup) 161
   juice, canned (1 glass) 170
Pumpkin pie (1 slice)................ 263

Name suggestions for boys

Aaron	Bradley	Dale	Gabriel	Irwin	Lambert
Abbott	Brendan	Dana	Garrett	Isaac	Lance
Abraham	Brett	Daniel	Garth	Ivan	Lawrence
Adam	Brian	Darryl	Gary		Lee
Adrian	Brooks	David	Geoffery	Jack	Leland
Alan	Bruce	Dennis	George	Jacob	Leo
Albert	Bryan	Derek	Gerald	Jamie	Leon
Alec	Burton	Donald	Gilbert	James	Leonard
Alex	Byron	Douglas	Giles	Jan	Leroy
Alexander		Drew	Glenn	Jared	Leslie
Alfred	Caleb	Dudley	Godfrey	Jason	Lester
Allen	Calvin	Duster	Gordon	Jasper	Levi
Alonzo	Cameron	Dustin	Graham	Jay	Lewis
Alphonse	Carl	Dwight	Grant	Jefferey	Lincoln
Andrew	Carter		Gregory	Jeremy	Lindsay
Angelo	Casey	Earl	Griffith	Jerome	Lionel
Anthony	Cedric	Edmund	Guy	Jesse	Llewellyn
Archibald	Charles	Edward		Joel	Lloyd
Ashley	Chester	Eli	Hal	John	Louis
Augustin	Christopher	Ellery	Hadley	Jonathan	Lowell
Austin	Clark	Elliott	Hamilton	Jordan	Lucas
Avery	Claude	Emerson	Harold	Joseph	Luke
	Clay	Emery	Harrison	Joshua	Luther
Baldwin	Clayton	Eric	Harry	Jules	Lyle
Barry	Clement	Ernest	Hartley	Julian	
Barth	Clifford	Ethan	Harvey	Justin	Mark
Barton	Clifton	Eugene	Harwood		Marlon
Baxter	Clinton	Evan	Henry	Karl	Marshall
Benjamin	Clyde	Everett	Herbert	Keith	Martin
Bennett	Cody	Ezra	Herman	Kelly	Marvin
Benedict	Conrad		Horace	Kenneth	Mason
Bernard	Cornelius	Fletcher	Howard	Kent	Matt
Bertram	Cory	Floyd	Hoyt	Kerry	Matthew
Blaine	Courtney	Forrest	Hugh	Kevin	Max
Blair	Craig	Foster	Humphrey	Kirby	Maxwell
Blake	Curtis	Frank		Kirk	Maynard
Boyd	Cyril	Franklin	Ian	Kit	Merlin
Bran	Cyrus	Frazer	Ira	Kurt	Melvin
Brad		Frederick	Irving	Kyle	Merrill
Bradford		Fremont			Michael

Mike
Millard
Milo
Milton
Mitchell
Monroe
Morgan
Morris
Murray
Myron

Nathan
Nathaniel
Neal
Ned
Neil
Nelson
Newton
Nicholas
Nick
Nigil
Noah
Noel
Nolan
Norbert
Norman
Norton

Olin
Oliver
Orlando
Orrin
Oscar
Otis
Owen

Parker
Parnell
Patrick

Patton
Paul
Penn
Perry
Peter
Phillip
Pierre
Prescot
Preston

Quentin
Quincy

Ralph
Ramon
Ramsey
Randall
Randolph
Raymond
Raynard
Reed
Reginald
Rex
Reynold
Richard
Robert
Robin
Rod
Roderick
Rodney
Roger
Roland
Ronald
Rory
Ross
Rowland
Roy
Rudolph

Rupert
Russell
Rutherford
Ryan

Salim
Sam
Sampson
Samuel
Sanders
Sandor
Sanford
Saul
Sawyer
Scott
Sean
Sebastian
Selby
Seth
Seward
Seymour
Shane
Shannon
Shawn
Shelby
Sheldon
Shelley
Sheridan
Sherman
Sherwin
Sherwood
Sidney
Siegfried
Silas
Simon
Sinclair
Slade
Sloan
Solomon
Spencer

Stacey
Stanford
Stanley
Stephen
Stewart
Stuart
Sumner
Sylvester

Tab
Tad
Talbot
Taylor
Terence
Terry
Thatcher
Thaddeus
Theodore
Thomas
Thorton
Thorpe
Thurston
Timmy
Timothy
Tobias
Toby
Todd
Tony
Torrance
Tracy
Travis
Trent
Trevor
Troy
Turner
Tyler
Tyrone

Ulysses
Upton

Van
Vance
Vaughn
Vern
Vernon
Victor
Vincent
Virgil

Wade
Wainwright
Wallace
Walter
Ward
Warner
Warren
Wayne
Webster
Wesley
Weston
Whitney
Wiley
Willard
William
Winfield
Winslow
Winston
Winthrop
Woodrow

Xavier
Yale
Yancy

Zachariah
Zachary
Zane

Name suggestions for girls

Abby	Bernadette	Christina	Edna	Gracie	Joanna
Abigail	Beth	Christine	Edwina	Gretchen	Joanne
Adair	Betsy	Cicely	Eileen	Gwendolyn	Jocelyn
Adele	Beverly	Claire	Elana	Gwyneth	Jodie
Adrienne	Bianca	Clara	Elise		Jordan
Aileen	Brandy	Clarissa	Elizabeth	Haley	Josephine
Alexandra	Brenda	Claudette	Ella	Hailey	Josie
Alexandria	Briana	Claudia	Ellen	Hannah	Joy
Alexis Alice	Bridget	Colette	Elsa	Hazel	Joyce
Alicia	Brigitte	Collen	Emily	Heather	Juanita
Allie	Brittany	Cordelia	Emma	Heidi	Judith
Allison	Brooke	Corey	Erica	Hilary	Judy
Allyn Alma		Courtney	Erin	Hilda	Julia
Alyssa	Caitlin	Crystal	Estelle	Holly	Julie
Amanda	Camille	Cybil	Esther	Ilene	June
Amber	Candace		Eva	Ina	Justine
Amelia	Cara	Dalila	Evelyn	Ines	
Amy	Carina	Dana	Faith	Ingrid	Kaitlyn
Andrea	Carla	Daniella	Felicia	Irene	Kala
Angela	Carlotta	Danielle	Fiona	Iris	Karen
Angelina	Carmen	Daphnie	Flora	Isabel	Kate
Anita	Carol	Daria	Florence	Isadora	Katherine
Ann	Caroline	Darla	Frances	Ivory	Kathleen
Anna	Carolyn	Dawn	Francine		Katie
Annabel	Carrie	Deanne	Francesca	Jacqueline	Katrina
Annette	Casey	Deborah		Jamie	Kayla
Antoinette	Cassandra	Delia	Gabriella	Jane	Kelley
April	Cassie	Denise	Gail	Janet	Kelsey
Ariel	Catherine	Desiree	Genevieve	Janice	Kendra
Ashley	Celeste	Diana	Georgeanne	Janis	Kim
Athena	Celia	Diane	Georgia	Jasmine	Kimberly
Aubrey	Charlene	Dolores	Georgiana	Jeanine	Kira
Audrey	Charlotte	Dominique	Gerri	Jeanette	Kirsten
Barbara	Charmaine	Donna	Gillian	Jennifer	Krista
Beatrice	Chelsea	Dorothy	Gina	Jenny	Kristin
Belinda	Cheryl	Drew	Ginger	Jessica	
Benita	Chloe		Giselle	Jill	Larissa
	Chloris	Ebony	Gloria	Jillian	Laura
	Christie	Edith	Grace	Joan	Lauren

Lauryn	Mary	Penny	Shirley	Violet
Leah	Marybeth	Phoebe	Shoshana	Virginia
Leigh	Maureen	Phylis	Simone	Vivian
Lena	Megan	Piper	Sondra	
Leslie	Melanie	Portia	Sonya	Wendy
Letitia	Melinda	Priscilla	Sophia	Whitney
Lila	Melissa		Sophie	Whilhelmina
Lilith	Mercedes	Rachel	Stacy	Winifred
Lillian	Mia	Ramona	Stephanie	Winona
Lily	Michele	Raquel	Susan	
Linda	Millicent	Raven	Suzanne	Yolanda
Lindsey	Miranda	Rebecca	Sybil	Yvette
Lisa	Monica	Regan	Sydney	Yvonne
Lola	Monique	Regina		
Lorelei	Morgan	Renee	Tabitha	Zelda
Loretta	Moria	Rhonda	Tamara	Zena
Lorna		Roberta	Tami	Zoe
Lorraine	Nadia	Robyn	Tammy	
Louisa	Nadine	Rona	Tanya	
Louise	Nancy	Rosa	Tara	
Lucia	Natalie	Rose	Teresa	
Lucille	Natasha	Rosemarie	Theresa	
Lucinda	Nicole	Ruth	Terese	
Lucy	Nina	Ruthann	Tess	
Lydia	Noel		Tessa	
Lynne	Nola	Sabrina	Tiffany	
	Nora	Samantha	Tina	
Madeline		Sandra	Terri	
Magdalena	Odelia	Sara	Toni	
Mandy	Olivia	Sarah	Tracy	
Marcella	Opal	Sarena	Tuesday	
Marcia		Sasha		
Margaret	Paige	Selina	Una	
Maria	Pamela	Shannon	Ursula	
Marie	Pat	Sharon		
Maribel	Patricia	Shawn	Valerie	
Marilyn	Paula	Sheila	Vanessa	
Marissa	Pauline	Shelly	Veronica	
Marlene	Penelope	Sheryl	Victoria	

Index

Questions for your clinician

_____

_____

_____

_____

_____

_____

_____

_____

_____

_____

_____

_____

_____

_____

Questions for your clinician

_____

_____

_____

_____

_____

_____

_____

_____

_____

_____

_____

_____

_____

_____

Notes

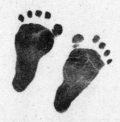

Other books in this series

A Miracle in the Making

Pregnancy and Childbirth*

A Doctor Discusses Nutrition During
Pregnancy and Breastfeeding

Breastfeeding

A Doctor Discusses Your Life
After the Baby is Born
The Postpartum Period

A Doctor Discusses the Care and
Development of Your Baby

A Doctor Discusses Menopause
and Current Estrogen Guidelines

A Doctor's Approach to Sensible
Dieting and Weight Control

Budlong minibooks

A Guide to Breast Health Care –
How to Examine Your Breasts*

STD's and Vaginitis

Osteoporosis – The Silent Stalker*

*Available in Spanish

BUDLONG PRESS, A CooperSurgical Company • Trumbull, CT 06611